The Mind of chipK:

I got into music at a pretty early age

The Mind of chipK:
Enter At Your Own Risk

A 45-day interactive devotional by
Chip Kendall from thebandwithnoname

Authentic

Cover design by River
Design and typesetting by Temple Design, Manchester
Print Management by Adare Carwin
Printed in Great Britain by J. H. Haynes & Co. Ltd., Sparkford

Contents

Thanks

Helen – my best friend and favourite typist.

My family – for always encouraging me and looking out for me.

thebandwithnoname – for all the fun memories (both old and new!).

Tim & Rach – my late night research team.

Doug-dog, Andy, Zulu, Zarc and Isaac – for help with the CD.

Sparky – for help with the cover, and loads of free work.

Mouse man – for help with the contract.

Nat – for all the last minute emergency e-mails.

Andy Hawthorne – for always providing words of wisdom.

The Everett family – for letting me use your laptop.

Paul Garrett – for the writeable CDs.

Andrea & Tom Baker – for the office space and help with pictures.

Matt Stubbs – the 'beautiful' typist.

Malcolm Down and everyone at Authentic – for all your wonderful ideas and creative input.

Angela Little – for her editorial work.

Rebecca St James – for writing *40 days with God* (the inspiration for this book!).

To everyone who features in the stories on these pages – you made it possible.

Lord Jesus – all this is for you. You are the source of every good thing in my life, and I am forever indebted to you.

To you, the reader – thanks for allowing God to minister to your soul through this book. Be inspired, challenged and encouraged to search the heart and mind of God. He has so many amazing plans for your life (Jeremiah 29:11), if only you'll open up and let him reveal them to you.

A boy and his dog – how sweet

Endorsements

'chipK is really one of my favourite people. Occasionally when I see him doing his slightly demented yet amazing stuff with thebandwithnoname I feel like the guy from Decca records who turned down the Beatles. My slightly dubious claim to fame is that I am the man who foolishly turned down chipK several years ago when he auditioned for our Message band, the Tribe. I've since found myself kicking myself regularly as I've seen chip develop into someone who is not only wonderful on stage but loves Jesus and his word with a passion.

That's why I'm so delighted to endorse this little book. It's authentic, it's challenging and because it's digging into God's life-changing Book, if you let it, it will completely change you.'

Andy Hawthorne, The Message

'More exclusive than a backstage pass to a TBWNN gig – chipK offers 'access all areas' into the crazy corridors of his mind! My advice is, expect the unexpected and get ready to be challenged to your core – this is a faith-journey you won't be forgetting in a hurry!'

Matt Wilson, The Message

'chipK's passion for God always screams from the stage and it does the same from the pages of his book.'

Mark Pennells, Director, Innervation Trust

'chipK's passion for God sets him apart from many of his peers and it's infectious. When he's around, you know it! His heart to help people, whether speaking from a stage or in a quiet conversation or even writing a book like this one, is all driven by his heart for Jesus.'

Mike Rimmer, Freelance Broadcaster and Journalist

'As he admits himself, chipK has never been one for doing things by halves. And it's Chip's brand of radical 'all or nothing' Christianity that makes sense in this age of vacuous believe-what-you-like spirituality. As this book spells out, Chip has got hold of the real deal where life becomes an exhilarating roller coaster ride of faith, miracles and supernaturally imparted peace and joy. Being a wrinkled slaphead you might think I would find little of interest in the youthful observations of a rock culture evangelist. Instead, I find myself encouraged and energised by Chip's pointers to Maximum Life.'

Tony Cummings, Cross Rhythms

Me and my sister next to our family altar in the Negev desert

Introduction

IMPORTANT INFORMATION!
THIS WILL HELP YOU UNDERSTAND THIS BOOK!

The book you're holding in your hands is an autobiographical interactive spiritual devotion journal. That means it's basically just a bunch of random stories from my life, meant to encourage, challenge and inspire you in your personal walk with God. Each entry has been broken down into three sections: chipK's mind, God's mind and your mind.

chipK's mind: This section will hopefully fill you in on some of my own experiences. Try not to laugh too much.

God's mind: This section will give you an idea of what God says in the Bible about whatever topic is under discussion. Always keep a Bible nearby in case you need to check out the context of these Scriptures.

your mind: This section is probably the most important. This is an opportunity to apply the stuff you've just read about in my life and in the Scriptures to your *own* life. You'll only get as much out of it as you put into it, so think long and hard before you fill in the blanks. Don't worry about trying to put in the 'right' answers. Just be honest. You might also want to discuss them with your parents or a youth leader.

Having spent a lot of time in both America and England, you'll quickly discover that I often use words and phrases you may not recognize. For this reason, I've included a short English–American dictionary at the back of the book. So any time you come across a word like 'naff' or 'vacation', just flip over to the back and educate yourself in transatlantic culture. It's all part of your journey into the mind of chipK.

Okay, you're almost ready to get started. Before you do, though, let me give you a brief overview of my extremely abnormal life. It should help all the stories to fall into place in your brain later on.

I was born in Gainesville, Florida exactly one week before Christmas, 1977. Since it was so near the big day, the nurse actually wrapped me up in a massive Christmas stocking before handing me over to my mom. Now, before you throw up from the cuteness of it all, let me assure you that this very same stocking was used for many years to come as my actual traditional stocking to be filled up by Santa every year. That's a lot of presents . . .

My very first stage performance was at the ripe old age of one week old. I appeared in the starring role of baby Jesus, alongside my very tired mother, Mary (really, that's her name) in our church's Christmas production. Obviously, I don't remember much from that first performance, but if it was anything like the way I perform with thebandwithnoname nowadays, then it wasn't a very silent night.

When I was 6 months old, we moved to Vero Beach, Florida. My sister was born there about a year later, and that's where we stayed until I was twelve. Looking back now, I'd say this was about as normal as my life ever got. We had a big house, two cars, satellite television and a dog. I went to school, belonged to a little league baseball team, had a very cool waterbed, and absolutely loved going to church. It was a pretty big church. There were two thousand members at one point. Dad was the worship pastor there and he loved to put on really extravagant musical productions. My sister and I always got the best roles in those productions . . . I wonder why.

Shortly before I experienced that indescribable greatness of becoming a teenager, we moved to Jerusalem, Israel. This is where I reckon things go slightly abnormal. Just when all my friends were heading to the dentist to get braces and learning to deal with zits, I was heading to the Middle East and learning to deal with the threat of war – plus having zits! It was the summer of 1990, and this mean-looking guy with a big moustache called Saddam was shouting abuse at the Israeli government. Nevertheless, all four of us felt a distinct call from God that we were to move to the Holy Land. So we did. We even took the dog with us.

I'll admit, it took me a good couple of years to adjust to my new life in Jerusalem. But throughout my teen years, God definitely had his hand on my life. My sister and I were home-schooled, and we spent up to half of each year travelling all over the world, ministering in churches as a family in around twenty-five different nations. We were like a four person tag-team, singing dancing preaching machine. I would inevitably perform a mime piece, my sister and I would perform a few tracks together, we'd all sing a couple more songs and my dad would preach about whatever God had laid on his heart. We even made a few albums together. During this time, I really got into songwriting and ended up making a couple of albums, one by myself, *Show Me Who I Am*, and one with my sister, *Back to the Drawing Board*.

When I was 19, I left home and moved to Pasadena, California to study mime, dance and the Bible. I lived there for three years and met loads of great, talented people, including a young lady from Gateshead, England. We were great friends for the first two years, and then, just before she moved back home to the UK, something happened. It was like a light switch went on. BING! I actually fell head over heels, madly in love with her. We dated long distance (she was in England and I was working as a PE teacher in California) over the next year or so, and in January 2000, I proposed to her on stage in front of two thousand Africans at the end of a mime piece we performed together in Kampala, Uganda. She said yes, and on 28 August 2000, I married my best friend, Helen.

Helen and I lived in the Byker Wall (a bit like the walls of Jericho, only not *quite* so exciting) in Newcastle-upon-Tyne, England, for a year, just working and getting used to actually being married to each other. Then we got the invitation to move down to Manchester and work with a new up-and-coming youth ministry called Innervation. Their vision is to see millions of young people become Christians and so they set up Christian bands to go into schools in the UK. They put me in their touring band, thebandwithnoname, and Helen has since become Assistant Director of the entire ministry.

That pretty much brings us up to where we're at now. We're constantly thrilled to see hundreds of young people becoming Christians at the gigs we participate in. God has yet to fulfil many of the prophetic words and prayers that have been spoken over this ministry, and we look forward to seeing them all come to pass.

Hope you enjoy the book.

CHANEL No. ALIVE

chipK's mind

We are the aroma of Christ

Ever smelled a dead rat? I have. I was cleaning out our backyard trash-can. It'd been left untouched for months and was filled with heaps of old rubbish and no small amount of rainwater. When I lifted the lid and began to tip out the water, the most horrific stench you can possibly imagine came gushing out. My wife Helen could even smell it from inside! It was absolutely puke-worthy; I never did find the actual rat, but the smell of it hung in my nose for the rest of the day.

According to the Bible, we Christians are the 'aroma of Christ'. That doesn't mean we physically smell like a Middle Eastern carpenter, but rather that we should have the same effect on the people around us as Jesus had on the people around him. To one kind of person Jesus smelled like that dead rat I mentioned earlier. To another, he smelled even better than that famous perfume – Chanel No.5. When we're living God's way, we smell as nice and clean as life itself . . . I guess you could call it 'Chanel No. Alive'!

So, what do people 'smell' when they hang around you? Are you really much of a threat to the devil? Or are you just a smelly dead rat?

God's mind

But thanks be to God, who always leads us in victory through Christ. God uses us to spread his knowledge everywhere like a sweet-smelling perfume. Our offering to God is this: we are the sweet smell of Christ among those who are being saved and among those who are being lost. To those who are lost, we are the smell of death that brings death, but to those who are being saved, we are the smell of life that brings life.
2 Corinthians 2:14–16a

Then the priests will burn these parts on the altar, on the whole burnt offering that is on the wood of the fire. It is an offering made by fire, and its smell is pleasing to the Lord.
Leviticus 3:5

A curse will be on anyone who doesn't do what the Lord says, and a curse will be on anyone who holds back his sword from killing. The people of Moab have never known trouble. They are like wine left to settle; they have never been poured from one jar to another. They have not been taken into captivity. So they taste as they did before, and their smell has not changed.
Jeremiah 48:10–11

We are the **smell of life** that brings life.

your mind

What are some of the foulest stenches I've ever smelled?

What do people 'smell' when they hang around me?

What are the advantages of smelling like Jesus?

And the disadvantages?

I could be a pleasing aroma to God today by:

15

The Mind of chipK

FEAR GOD

chipK's mind

Nobody likes to be sent to the principal's office – unless, of course, you are receiving some sort of award. Nobody likes getting all dressed up for weddings – unless, of course, you're a girl. Nobody likes standing before a judge in a court of law – unless, of course, you've just been proven innocent.

So why do we do all these things anyway? Out of reverence and respect, that's why. That principal has the authority to kick you out of school, if he chooses. That bride and groom are about to promise the rest of their lives to each other. That judge has enough credentials to put you in the slammer for life.

Fearing God means showing respect

Sadly, some people misunderstand the phrase, 'the fear of the Lord'. They think it means that you should be afraid of God, as if he's about to strike you with lightning or something terrible like that. This couldn't be further from the truth. Fearing God simply means showing respect where it's due. Give honour to your creator Father who holds the universe in the palm of his powerful yet gentle hand. Have a bit of reverence for him next time you set foot into his presence, but don't be afraid.

After all, the cross of Jesus has already proved your innocence.

God's mind

Knowledge begins with respect for the Lord, but fools hate wisdom and self-control.
Proverbs 1:7

Respect for the Lord will teach you wisdom. If you want to be honoured, you must be humble.
Proverbs 15:33

Remember your Creator while you are young, before the days of trouble come and the years when you say, 'I find no pleasure in them . . . Now, everything has been heard, so I give my final advice: honour God and obey his commands, because this is all people must do.
Ecclesiastes 12:1,13

Respect for the Lord will teach you **wisdom**

your mind

Who else do I show respect for (besides God)?

When do I find that I'm afraid of God? Why is this?

How do I practically show my respect for God?

Which of these positions demonstrates reverence?

- ○ **Sitting**
- ○ **Standing**
- ○ **Kneeling**
- ○ **Lying on back**
- ○ **Lying on front**
- ○ **Crouching**
- ○ **Slouching**
- ○ **Kneeling on one leg**
- ○ **Arms raised**
- ○ **Head lowered**
- ○ **Arms folded**
- ○ **Head stand**

TREASURE

chipK's mind

thebandwithnoname has done countless interviews over the years, and we've been asked pretty much every question under the sun. 'How did you get your weird name?' 'How would you describe your music?' 'Who do you think would win in a battle between Superman, Batman and Spiderman?' I remember one question that particularly threw all of us for a loop. It's a simple question, really. 'What is your most prized possession?' After a fairly long pause, I think we all agreed that the thing we each most treasured was our cell phone. Accidentally leaving our cell phone at home was, at best, extremely painful, and to actually lose one altogether would be outright traumatic. But long after the interview was over, this question still haunted me. What do I truly treasure the most?

At the end of the day, it's really all just stuff

Nowadays, people make all sorts of things their *treasure*: money, cars, houses, CDs, laptops, video games . . . But at the end of the day, it's really all just *stuff*. You won't be able to take 'stuff' with you to heaven when your human body dies. It's all man-made foolish nonsense, stuck to this life like the world's strongest magnet. That's why Jesus says it's much better to store up treasure in heaven, where we can be sure it'll never decay or get stolen. How do we do that? By doing things that have eternal significance, like leading people to Jesus, or getting to know God better through prayer and reading the Bible, or even just being generous with our time, money and 'stuff'.

These are the kind of things I hope to take with me to heaven, not my Nokia.

God's mind

'Don't store treasure for yourselves here on earth where moths and rust will destroy them and thieves can break in and steal them. But store your treasures in heaven where they cannot be destroyed by moths or rust and where thieves cannot break in and steal them. Your heart will be where your treasure is.'
Matthew 6:19–21

'Don't worry and say, "What will we eat?" or "What will we drink?" or "What will we wear?" The people who don't know God keep trying to get these things, and your Father in heaven knows you need them. The thing you should want most is God's kingdom and doing what God wants. Then all these other things you need will be given to you.
Matthew 6:31–33

Think only about the things in heaven, not the things on earth.
Colossians 3:2

Jesus sat near the Temple money box and watched the people put in their money. Many rich people gave large sums of money. Then a poor widow came and put in two very small copper coins, which were not even worth a penny. Calling his followers to him, Jesus said, 'I tell you the truth, this poor widow gave more than all those rich people. They gave only what they did not need. This woman is very poor, but she gave all she had; she gave all she had to live on.'
Mark 12:41–44

your mind

TREASURE

What is my most prized possession?

I will show my generosity by giving away two things today:

1.

2.

What are some other ways I can store up treasures in heaven?

When I go to heaven, what *will* I be able to take with me? (HINT: John 17:3)

CONTENTMENT

chipK's mind

When I was growing up in Jerusalem, things weren't always peachy. Being an American teenager with an American appetite stuck in a Middle Eastern world of veggie salads and kosher meat, proved to be quite difficult at times. I'd gone from 'dessert' food to 'desert' food and, trust me, I was gagging for that missing 's'.

My parents, my sister and I firmly believed that God had called us to live by faith, so we moved to Jerusalem with no promise of a pay cheque for my dad, just a bunch of friends and family pledging support from 'the land of plenty' back home.

Am I going to groan, or am I going to grow?

I remember one evening our cupboards were literally bare. At the dinner table Mom asked us, 'Have you heard of the Last Supper?' 'Yes,' we all replied. 'Well, you're eating it!' Miraculously, a bit of dosh arrived the next day from one of our supporters who said she'd had a dream that we'd run out of food and wound up eating 'bug sandwiches'. That money covered our next day's food budget, so thankfully the dream never came true!

That was an extreme example of a missionary family learning to trust God to provide their needs. But I think it was also a good lesson in contentment. To be honest with you, I'm still learning that same lesson. I'm faced with situations every day when I have to decide between complaining or choosing to be content. Am I going to groan, or am I going to grow? A great way to battle the moan of what you ain't got is to remind yourself of what you do got.

Anyone up for a bug sandwich?

God's mind

I am not telling you this because I need anything. I have learned to be satisfied with the things I have and with everything that happens. I know how to live when I am poor, and I know how to live when I have plenty. I have learned the secret of being happy at any time in everything that happens, when I have enough to eat and when I go hungry, when I have more than I need and when I do not have enough. I can do all things through Christ, because he gives me strength.
Philippians 4:11–13

Do everything without complaining or arguing. Then you will be innocent and without any wrong. You will be God's children without fault. But you are living with crooked and evil people all around you, among whom you shine like stars in the dark world. You offer the teaching that gives life. So when Christ comes again, I can be happy because my work was not wasted. I ran the race and won.
Philippians 2:14–16

'Give us the food we need for each day.'
Matthew 6:11

Give us the **food** we need for **each day**

your mind

One thing I wish I had, but I don't:

Three things I've got that I'm thankful for:

1.

2.

3.

What do I complain the most about?

Why is it easier to groan than it is to grow?

GOD'S BIGGEST ADJECTIVE

chipK's mind

Think about this for a second. If you had to think of one word which best describes God, what would it be? What's the biggest, most defining characteristic he possesses? How would you pack all the awesome wonderfulness of the almighty creator of the universe into just a single adjective? Would it be 'love'? That's a pretty deep, meaningful, simple-yet-at-the-same-time-complex kind of word. How about 'faithful'? There have certainly been a lot of famous songs written about that one. Or what about something a bit more abstract, like 'onion'? Anyone who's seen *Shrek* will know what I'm talking about.

We humans just can't get enough of it!

If you check the Bible, you'll find that actually the most common adjective used to describe God isn't any of these. It's 'holy'. God is ultimately, perfectly and unquestionably holy. That means totally set apart and unlike anything else that squirms, blossoms, shines, twirls, sits, poops or pees in the entire universe. God's holiness is something we could spend an eternity exploring and digesting. In fact, we will! That's why John's vision of heaven in the book of Revelation includes those huge weird-looking creatures surrounding God's throne shouting, 'Holy, holy, holy!' over and over again. And we humans just can't get enough of it!

Now think about this. God tells us to be holy as *he* is holy. (*Holy moly!*)

God's mind

your mind

Then God said, 'Do not come any closer. Take off your sandals, because you are standing on holy ground. I am the God of your ancestors – the God of Abraham, the God of Isaac and the God of Jacob.' Moses covered his face because he was afraid to look at God.
Exodus 3:5–6

'I am the Lord your God. Keep yourselves holy for me because I am holy. Don't make yourselves unclean with any of these crawling animals.'
Leviticus 11:44

Each of these four living creatures had six wings and was covered all over with eyes, inside and out. Day and night they never stop saying: 'Holy, holy, holy is the Lord God Almighty. He was, he is, and he is coming.'
Revelation 4:8

Keep yourselves **holy** for me because **I am holy**

If I had to describe myself in one word, what would it be?

How is being holy different from just being odd?

When am I most aware of God's holiness in my life?

How can I practise being holy in the same way that God is holy?

PHONE HOME

chipK's mind

Don't you just hate it when your cell phone runs out of credit? Your best friend was just about to tell you the best part of the story, and now you've got to wait until you can buy another phone card to call them back.

Well, what if I was to tell you about a cell phone that never runs out of credit, costs absolutely nothing for both peak and off-peak minutes and, best of all, it still works even in places where there's no network coverage! You'd stand in line for hours to get your hands on one of those babies, wouldn't you? Prayer is a lot like this miracle phone. It allows us free access to the throne room of God himself, and it's available 24–7, no matter where we're 'calling' from. God wants us to talk to him just the way we are. No big fancy words, no poetic rhymes, no tremendous reports on how we solved the world's hunger problem. He just wants us to be ourselves. You know what else? More often than not, he wants to talk back to us. Not just through the Bible and other people, but also straight to our hearts. He loves to remind us how much he cares for us, especially during the toughest moments of our day.

He wants us to be ourselves

Why not take a few minutes right now to just close your eyes and talk with God. You can even use your cell phone if you want. Tell him how you're feeling and what's weighing heavy on your mind. Then spend some time just listening to what he's saying back. You don't have to worry about wasting any phone credit if there's a long pause.

And heaven's always got full network coverage.

God's mind

God, your thoughts are precious to me. They are so many!
Psalm 139:17

Pray in the Spirit at all times with all kinds of prayers, asking for everything you need. To do this you must always be ready and never give up. Always pray for all God's people.'
Ephesians 6:18

Pray continually.
1 Thessalonians 5: 17

'When you pray, don't be like the hypocrites. They love to stand in the synagogues and on the street corners and pray so people will see them. I tell you the truth, they already have their full reward. When you pray, you should go into your room and close the door and pray to your Father who cannot be seen. Your Father can see what is done in secret, and he will reward you. And when you pray, don't be like those people who don't know God. They continue saying things that mean nothing, thinking that God will hear them because of their many words. Don't be like them, because your Father knows the things you need before you ask him. So when you pray, you should pray like this: "Our Father in heaven, may your name always be kept holy. May your kingdom come and what you want be done, here on earth as it is in heaven. Give us the food we need for each day. Forgive us our sins, just as we have forgiven those who sinned against us. And do not cause us to be tempted, but save us from the Evil One."'
Matthew 6:5–13

When a believing person prays, great things happen.
James 5:16b

your mind

What's the longest I've ever prayed?

What's the longest I've ever gone without praying?

What do I feel like in times when I've neglected talking to God?

In what ways do I know God is listening to me and answering my prayers?

What are four things I can pray for right now?

1.

2.

3.

4.

Now do it!

UNDER CONSTRUCTION

chipK's mind

When I was 6 years old, I was utterly convinced that I could fly. The potential was inside me and, as far as I was concerned, all I needed was a little practise. So, one afternoon, I went outside and built a makeshift ramp out of scrap pieces of wood (at this time we were in the process of building my mom's dream home, so our 'house' was really more of a construction site than a home). Over and over I'd run up the ramp, jump off and sadly, but soundly, land with a thud on the grass at the other end. Undeterred, I'd dust myself off and start again, all the while entertaining imaginations of myself flying past my mom's window shouting, 'Look Mom, I'm flying!'

'Look Mom, I'm flying!'

As much as I'd love to tell you that in the end I achieved my superman status, I cannot. In fact, quite the opposite occurred. On one jump I managed to land slightly too close to the construction site. I can still remember the agonising pain shooting through my body as my foot landed on an old rusty nail. As blood gushed out, my mom got quite a different shock from the one I'd been imagining, just minutes earlier.

Sometimes it doesn't take much to humbly bring you back down to earth when your head's up in the clouds. One minute you're full of faith and confidence and it seems like nothing can stop you, then your humanity kicks in. Doubt and frustration have a way of making everything seem so painful and ridiculous, like that nail in my foot. In times like these, the best place to go is straight into the arms of your heavenly Father. Nothing fazes him.

Not even old rusty nails.

God's mind

'I told you these things so that you can have peace in me. In this world you will have trouble, but be brave! I have defeated the world.'
John 16:33

The Spirit we received does not make us slaves again to fear: it makes us children of God. With that Spirit we cry out, 'Father'. And the Spirit himself joins with our spirits to say we are God's children. If we are God's children, we will receive blessings from God together with Christ. But we must suffer as Christ suffered so that we will have glory as Christ has glory.
Romans 8:15–17

We also have joy with our troubles, because we know that these troubles produce patience. And patience produces character, and character produces hope. And this hope will never disappoint us, because God has poured out his love to fill our hearts. He gave us his love through the Holy Spirit, whom God has given to us.
Romans 5:3–5

God began doing a good work in you, and I am sure he will continue it until it is finished when Jesus Christ comes again.
Philippians 1:6

Patience produces **character,** and character produces **hope**

your mind

What's the most foolish thing I've ever done?

How did it make me feel?

In what ways am I still 'under construction'?

What are three things my heavenly Father can offer me that no one else can?

1.

2.

3.

27

The Mind of chipK

SERVANTHOOD

chipK's mind

One of the toughest things to maintain when I'm out on the road with thebandwithnoname is an attitude of service. I'm constantly reminding myself that I'm there to serve – not just the organizers of the event, but also my fellow band members and even the people who are just there to enjoy the show. There are many examples in the Bible of what it means to be a servant – heroes like Joseph, Daniel, Ruth and Onesimus. Jesus can be seen washing his disciples' feet, a job usually done by the household slave of his time. But I'd like to tell you about a modern day servant-hero who I've come across in my travels. His name is Charles.

> **I'm constantly reminding myself that I'm there to serve**

Charles is a retired solicitor who lives in Tunbridge Wells, UK. He has a lovely wife, grown-up kids, a very nice big house and a posh English accent. He's extremely 'well read' and at the end of every conversation I have with him, I always feel smarter than I did before. But the coolest thing I've learned about Charles is his willingness to serve. He's always been a tuxedo-wearing steward at the gigs we've done in his area, helping out wherever he's needed the most. And at the last 'GrassRootz' festival we played, he was found picking up litter all over the muddy campsite. Just imagine, a posh, retired solicitor bent over, scooping up dirty, wet rubbish!

That's what I want to be like. That's what Jesus asks all of us to be like. That's what I call a servant.

God's mind

Jesus called all the followers together and said, 'You know that the rulers of the non-Jewish people love to show their power over the people. And their important leaders love to use all their authority. But it should not be that way among you. Whoever wants to become great among you must serve the rest of you like a servant. Whoever wants to become first among you must serve the rest of you like a slave. In the same way, the Son of Man did not come to be served. He came to serve others and to give his life as a ransom for many people.'
Matthew 20:25–28

Jesus' followers began to have an argument about which one of them was the greatest. Jesus knew what they were thinking, so he took a little child and stood the child beside him. Then Jesus said, 'Whoever accepts this little child in my name accepts me. And whoever accepts me accepts the One who sent me, because whoever is least among you all is really the greatest.'
Luke 9:46–48

When he had finished washing their feet, he put on his clothes and sat down again. He asked, 'Do you understand what I have just done for you? You call me "Teacher" and "Lord", and you are right, because that is what I am. If I, your Lord and Teacher, have washed your feet, you also should wash each other's feet. I did this as an example so that you should do as I have done for you. I tell you the truth, a servant is not greater than his master. A messenger is not

greater than the one who sent him. If you know these things, you will be happy if you do them.'
John 13:12–17

Anyone who has the gift of serving should serve.
Romans 12:7a

your mind

Who has God called me to serve?

Where are my services needed the most?

Who do I know who's a real servant?

I will serve those around me today by:

FRUIT

chipK's mind

When my wife and I first moved to the Manchester area we rented a small house with a massive garden at the back. In the centre of the garden stood an old apple tree. It wasn't long before the novelty of having a real fruit tree in our garden wore off, though, as we quickly discovered it was totally rotten. It only produced rotten apples! The grass was always covered with 'em, and we had to continually gather them up before they attracted rats. Our beloved fruit tree was only delivering false promises.

You can spot a good one by the fruit they produce

One day, there was a light tapping on our front door. It was a handful of kids from the neighbourhood. 'Can we pick apples from your tree?' 'Sure!' we replied. At least it would save us having to pick them up once they'd fallen off the tree. A couple of hours went by and the tapping on our door returned. 'Your tree's fallen down,' they said. Somehow I couldn't believe it had fallen down all by itself . . .

Jesus said that people are a lot like trees. Only instead of producing fruits like apples, pears and oranges, people produce fruits of love, joy, peace and so on. You can spot a good one a mile away simply by the fruit they produce. Unfortunately, that's also how you spot a rotten one – by the fruit they don't produce.

The only thing they're useful for is attracting rats.

God's mind

'Be careful of false prophets. They come to you looking gentle like sheep, but they are really dangerous like wolves. You will know these people by what they do. Grapes don't come from thorn-bushes, and figs don't come from thorny weeds. In the same way, every good tree produces good fruit, but a bad tree produces bad fruit. A good tree cannot produce bad fruit, and a bad tree cannot produce good fruit. Every tree that does not produce good fruit is cut down and thrown into the fire. In the same way, you will know these false prophets by what they do. Not all those who say that I am their Lord will enter the kingdom of heaven. The only people who will enter the kingdom of heaven are those who do what my Father in heaven wants. On the last day many people will say to me, "Lord, Lord, we spoke for you, and through you we forced out demons and did many miracles." Then I will tell them clearly, "Get away from me, you who do evil. I never knew you."'
Matthew 7:15–23

The wrong things the sinful self does are clear: being sexually unfaithful, not being pure, taking part in sexual sins, worshipping gods, doing witchcraft, hating, making trouble, being jealous, being angry, being selfish, making people angry with each other, causing divisions among people, feeling envy, being drunk, having wild and wasteful parties, and doing other things like these. I warn you now as I warned you before: those who do these things will not inherit God's kingdom. But the Spirit produces the fruit of love, joy, peace, patience, kindness, goodness, faithfulness, gentleness, self-control. There is no law that says these things are wrong.
Galatians 5:19–23

your mind

What is my favourite fruit?

If someone 'picked my fruit' what would they find?

What else can I learn about a tree by its roots? What do my 'roots' tell me about the kind of person I am?

What are three qualities every piece of good fruit always has?

1. Enough seeds to reproduce itself at least once.

2.

3.

PATIENCE

chipK's mind

We live in an age when practically everything is instant. Want food? Get fast food. Want the Web? Get broadband. Want conversation? Grab your mobile. The list goes on forever. But we all know what happens when things don't come instantly. Think about McDonald's. All of a sudden we become poor helpless victims, doomed to spend a whole fifteen minutes actually *waiting* for our fast food Big Mac. Then, when we try to make the most of this traumatic ordeal by texting a mate, we discover that the predictive text isn't working and it makes us want to scream. If this makes us late for our express train home, then, obviously, the entire day has been completely ruined! But as Christians, we've got an alternative to getting stressed, depressed or furious. When the Holy Spirit controls our lives, we can exercise *patience*.

What happens when things don't come instantly?

The best example we've got of someone having a massive dose of patience in the midst of hugely stressful situations is God himself. Think of how many times you've screwed up in your lifetime. Now multiply that by the amount of people in the whole world. Now multiply that by the amount of people who have ever lived (or ever *will* live for that matter) and you've got a good idea of how patient God is with us. He never stops loving us to maturity, like the world's best dad, watching and waiting as his kids grow up.

Just something to keep in mind next time you're tempted to bite someone's head off, when you'd rather be biting into a Big Mac.

God's mind

God has chosen you and made you his holy people. He loves you. So always do these things: show mercy to others, be kind, humble gentle and patient.
Colossians 3:12

But the Spirit produces the fruit of love, joy, peace, patience, kindness, goodness, faithfulness, gentleness, self-control.
Galatians 5:22-23a

It is the same way with God. He wanted to show his anger and to let people see his power. But he patiently stayed with those people he was angry with – people who were due to be destroyed.
Romans 9:22

But the people who trust the Lord will become strong again. They will rise up as an eagle in the sky; they will run and not need rest; they will walk and not become tired.
Isaiah 40:31

He **patiently** stayed with those people he was **angry** with

your mind

How long would I be willing to sit in a doctor's waiting room, listening for my name to be called?

How long would I be willing to sit quietly in God's presence, listening for his voice?

When are the times it's most difficult for me to be patient?

One situation in which God has been patient with me this past week is:

PATIENCE

GUARDING YOUR MIND

chipK's mind

Wise little sayings are everywhere. Somehow, throughout history, these ancient proverbs get recycled and continue to turn truths into simple bitesize easy-to-remember phrases. Take for instance, 'A watched pot never boils,' or 'An apple a day keeps the doctor away,' or 'If you sprinkle when you tinkle be a sweetie and wipe the seatie.' Truly educational.

'As a man thinks in his heart, so shall he be'

One of my favourite wise sayings, especially when it comes to guarding your mind, is this: 'Garbage in, garbage out.' Simple, but incredibly effective. Someone else said something very similar ages ago. He said, 'As a man thinks in his heart, so shall he be.' By saying this, he wasn't implying that if you think about carrots long enough you'll eventually turn into a carrot. He was talking about something much deeper than that. Whatever you spend most of your time thinking about, whether on a conscious level or even subconsciously, it's probably going to come out in your actions. If you fill your mind with sinful thoughts, guess what? You're gonna wind up sinning. Garbage in, garbage out. If you fill your mind with Scripture, you're going to start living according to the Bible.

By keeping tabs on what you feed your mind every day, you're also investing in a life that will lead to better rewards from your actions.

34

God's mind

Brothers and sisters, think about the things that are good and worthy of praise. Think about the things that are true and honourable and right and pure and beautiful and respected.
Philippians 4:8

'You have heard that it was said, "You must not be guilty of adultery". But I tell you that if anyone looks at a woman and wants to sin sexually with her, in his mind he has already done that sin with the woman.'
Matthew 5:27–28

'But what people say with their mouths comes from the way they think; these are the things that make people unclean. Out of the mind come evil thoughts, murder, adultery, sexual sins, stealing, lying and speaking evil of others. These things make people unclean; eating with unwashed hands does not make them unclean.'
Matthew 15:18–20

Do not change yourselves to be like the people of this world, but be changed within by a new way of thinking. Then you will be able to decide what God wants for you; you will know what is good and pleasing to him and what is perfect.
Romans 12:2

Do not be fooled: you cannot cheat God. People harvest only what they plant. If they plant to satisfy their sinful selves, their sinful selves will bring them ruin. But if they plant to please the Spirit, they will receive eternal life from the Spirit. We must not become tired of doing good. We will receive our harvest of eternal life at the right time if we do not give up.
Galatians 6:7–9

I stay awake all night so I can think about your promises.
Psalm 119:148

your mind

How would I describe the majority of my thought life?

Why is it important for me to guard my mind?

How do films, music and television affect the way I think?

What can I do to keep better tabs on what I think about?

The Mind of chipK

LOST and FOUND

chipK's mind

One of my favourite scenes in *The Lord of the Rings* trilogy takes place in the final movie, *Return of the King*.

> Location: Top of Mount Doom
> Characters: Frodo, Sam and Gollum
> Purpose: To destroy the ring

After having journeyed so far with Frodo, protecting him, and even carrying him along the way, Sam must watch in horror as Frodo and Gollum fight for possession of the ring. It was such a battle just to get this far, and now that it finally came right down to it, Frodo couldn't let go of the very thing that was destroying him. Gollum proves to be the greedier of the two, as he bites the ring (and finger!) off Frodo's hand, falls into the hot molten lava, and finally dies with an evil grin on his face. Without the lure of the ring to distract him, Frodo finally comes to his senses and narrowly escapes with Sam to a new world and a new life.

As a Christian, I'm meant to lose my life in order to find it. That means letting go of my way of doing things in exchange for a relationship with Jesus. But, like Frodo and his ring, sometimes it's not so easy to throw down the things that mean so much to me. As Gollum would say, they're just too *precious* to me. And even though he loves me more than I know, even Jesus (like Sam) cannot make the decision for me.

I must be determined to chuck my ring into the fire, and by doing so I can start a new life with the one who's been protecting and carrying me all along.

God's mind

'Those who love their lives will lose them, but those who hate their lives in this world will keep true life forever.'
John 12:25

I have wandered like a lost sheep. Look for your servant, because I have not forgotten your commands.
Psalm 119:176

'Suppose one of you has 100 sheep but loses one of them. Then he will leave the other 99 sheep in the open field and go out and look for the lost sheep until he finds it. And when he finds it, he happily puts it on his shoulders and goes home. He calls to his friends and neighbours and says, "Be happy with me because I have found my lost sheep." In the same way, I tell you there is more joy in heaven over one sinner who changes his heart and life, than over 99 good people who don't need to change.'
Luke 15:4–7

Those who **hate** their lives in this world will keep **true life** forever

your mind

How would I describe my relationship with Jesus at the moment?

What is the 'ring' I often hold on to (my way of doing things)? Be specific:

Three practical ways to lose my life in this world:

1.

2.

3.

OBEDIENCE

chipK's mind

I believe there's one thing every young boy needs. A dog. Mine was called 'Buddy' (we named him after our pastor in Florida . . . he wasn't too happy about that . . . the pastor, that is), and Buddy was half cocker spaniel and half poodle. He was a 'cock-a-poo'. It was a big responsibility having a dog to walk and clean and feed, but the rewards certainly outweighed the burdens. He was always there to welcome me home, make me smile and cheer me up when I was grumpy. Buddy was especially fun to wind up. The mere mention of the word 'cat' would set him off barking, jumping and generally going berserk. Eventually, he even learned the word in Hebrew, 'khatool', and this too would drive him crazy. Ah, those were the days!

When he started to get old, Buddy really struggled with one essential quality. Obedience. Now don't get me wrong, it wasn't on purpose. He was the most faithful friend a boy could ask for. Buddy's disobedience was due to the fact that he was almost entirely deaf! In fact, not only was he deaf, he suffered from terribly poor eyesight and a nasty recurring skin disease. So when we'd call him over for his skin medicine, we'd have to shout just to get him to hear us. Then, when he finally heard us, because of his bad eyesight, he'd run in the opposite direction!

The Bible tells a story about a guy called Jonah who kinda did the same thing to God. Only this dude wasn't blind or deaf. He knew beyond a doubt that God was calling him to go preach in a town called Nineveh, but he desperately did not want to go. So, like Buddy, he went in the opposite direction. After getting swallowed by a massive fish, he eventually sorted things out with God and went to Nineveh.

Obeying God is always the right thing to do. It's even better than giving up everything for him.

Ultimately, he's got your best interests at heart, and he knows what you need better than you do. Listen and obey.

God's mind

Story of Jonah
Jonah 1–3

But Samuel answered, 'What pleases the Lord more: burnt offerings and sacrifices or obedience to his voice? It is better to obey than to sacrifice. It is better to listen to God than to offer the fat of rams.'
1 Samuel 15:22–23a

Children, obey your parents as the Lord wants, because this is the right thing to do. The command says, 'Honour your father and mother.' This is the first command that has a promise with it– Then everything will be well with you, and you will have a long life on the earth.
Ephesians 6:1–3

Lord, teach me what you want me to do, and I will live by your truth. Teach me to respect you completely.
Psalm 86:11

It is better to **obey** than to sacrifice

your mind

On a scale of 1–10, how good am I at obeying my parents?

1   2   3   4   5   6   7   8   9   10

Are there any circumstances in my life today in which I'm not being obedient to God?

What happens when I *dis*obey God?

When was the last time I struggled with doing something I shouldn't have done?

What is God calling me to do *now*?

I will be obedient by:

LEAP OF FAITH

chipK's mind

I love kids. My friend, Isaac Porter, who's only 5 years old, is one of the most faith-filled people I've ever met. He fears nothing.

One day, I was at Isaac's house along with some of his friends, playing 'fort'. You know, when you take all the cushions off every sofa in the house and pile them into a massive structure for the sole purpose of sitting inside and staring at each other. Well, that's what we did. Once I managed to get all the kids inside, I started tapping on the 'roof', pretending to be the rain. It wasn't long before the rain got a bit more intense and turned into a thunderstorm, then the thunderstorm into hail, and then the hail into an all-out hurricane, collapsing the fort all around the squealing kids. They loved it!

Isaac jumped out of the fort shouting, 'My turn!' Once we'd rebuilt it, he proceeded to join me as the rain, thunderstorm and hail. But when it came time for the big finale I was surprised to see Isaac walk away, heading towards the other side of the room. And that's when it happened. Before I could say anything, he whirled round and started running at full speed, straight at us. The last thing I heard was, 'Here comes the hurricane!' as he hurled himself over the sofa, high into the air and crashed right through the roof of our fort! Unfortunately, he managed to find the exact spot where there were no pillows, people or playthings to cushion his blow, so he hit the floor pretty hard. He was hurt, but he felt a lot better once his mum came to the rescue.

Jesus once said that in order to be a part of his kingdom, we have to become like children. It's an upside-down kingdom, where the first is last, the last is first, the smallest is the biggest and the greatest is the servant of all. And somehow, when you really think about it, that makes a heck of a lot more sense. Especially when it comes to having faith in something. The older you get, the more baggage you take on; the more baggage you take on, the more you need to rely on that baggage to get you through life; the more you rely on that, the less you rely on God. Now, in Isaac's case, it probably wasn't the best idea to have *quite* so much faith in that fort. Thankfully (for us), God is a lot more dependable. Fact is, if we'll just drop our baggage and have child-like faith, God will always come to our rescue . . .

Even in our *hurricane*.

God's mind

Faith means being sure of the things we hope for and knowing that something is real even if we do not see it. Faith is the reason we remember great people who lived in the past. It is by faith we understand that the whole world was made by God's command so what we see was made by something that cannot be seen.
Hebrews 11:1–3

Then the people brought their little children to Jesus so he could put his hands on them and pray for them. His followers told them to stop, but Jesus said, 'Let the little children come to me. Don't stop them, because the kingdom of heaven belongs to people who are like these children.' After Jesus put his hands on the children, he left that place.
Matthew 19:13–15

Jesus answered, 'Because your faith is too small. I tell you the truth, if your faith is as big as a mustard seed, you can say to this mountain, "Move from here to there," and it will move. All things will be possible for you.'
Matthew 17:20

The Good News shows how God makes people right with himself – that it begins and ends with faith. As the Scripture says, 'But those who are right with God will live by trusting in him.'
Romans 1:17

your mind

Who do I know that has *a lot* of faith?

What is some of the baggage stopping me from having child-like faith?

When's the last time I took a real 'leap of faith'?

5 things I can do if I start to have doubts about what I believe:

1.

2.

3.

4.

5.

SPACE BOWL

chipK's mind

I'll be the first to admit, water slides can sometimes be extremely naff. Especially in England. I mean, in the States we don't mess around when it comes to theme parks and water slides, but over in England it's a different story. There is one exception though, which I discovered quite recently. Butlins' very own . . . *Space Bowl* . . . (please provide echo). This is the closest feeling to being flushed down the toilet you will ever experience. After blazing through a series of twists and turns, you hurtle into a massive bowl at the speed of light. Then, depending on how heavy you are, you're sent whirling around the curve of the bowl, before plunging through the massive hole in the middle and drowning in a six-foot pool of water! With a full-on waterfall gushing down the hole past you, it's almost impossible not to swallow a lungful. I did. Twice. It wasn't very nice.

The closest thing to being flushed down the toilet you will ever experience

So many times we can start to give in to peer pressure, just like the *Space Bowl* experience. What starts out as a fun idea turns into a downward spiralling of bad addictions and we eventually fall helplessly into a pool of misery. How many 'lungfuls' of pride must I swallow, before I recognize that God made me to be the person I am, not what the people around me influence me to be? We need to be more like those three Hebrew guys in the book of Daniel who refused to bow to the king's statue, even though everyone else around them was doing it. We can stand up for what we believe in, even if it means being unpopular.

Trust me, it's better than being flushed down a toilet!

God's mind

Story of three Hebrew guys.
Daniel 3

Do not change yourselves to be like the people of this world, but be changed within by a new way of thinking.
Romans 12:2a

I praise you because you made me in an amazing and wonderful way. What you have done is wonderful. I know this very well.
Psalm 139:14

Do not change yourselves to be like the people of this world, but **be changed within** by a new way of thinking

your mind

What's the most ridiculous thing I've done in order to be popular?

What have I done that might be considered extremely unpopular?

How would Jesus handle peer pressure?

What are some real practical ways I can combat peer pressure by standing up for what I believe?

that's me!

My youth group in Jerusalem

family K.
Left to right: Marianne (Sis), Roy (Dad), Helen, Mary (Mom), me

My beautiful wife and I strike our best Tribe pose

Day 73: Fox's Glacier, New Zealand. Two arctic voyagers scout the icy terrain... (whilst freezing their butts off)

SECRET INGREDIENT

chipK's mind

Having spent my childhood under the hot and humid Florida sun, I am a huge fan of the most refreshing, thirst-quenching beverage ever invented by mankind. Of course, I speak of none other than . . . the slushy. I've thoroughly enjoyed many of them over the years, but one slushy in particular will always remain especially memorable to me. This one had a secret ingredient.

Now, it's important for me to first explain that in the States we do slushies slightly differently than in the UK. Everything's bigger in America, and our slushies are no exception. In order to cram the maximum slush into your cup, they add a curved lid (a bit like a McDonald's McFlurry) with a hole in the top just big enough for the straw. This makes it more difficult to see into the cup, but then again, why would you need to *look* at something that *tastes* so heavenly?

Anyway, back to my story. I remember sucking along quite happily on my slushy until a chunk of ice stopped up the straw. No problem. A few quick stabs with my straw, and I was back to my happy sucking. Then I hit the chunk of ice again. So I gave it another few stabs, and went back to sucking. Then it happened again. The cycle of sucking, stopping, stabbing, and back to sucking again repeated itself over and over, until eventually I was convinced that the only thing left in my cup was this annoying chunk of ice.

I wanted my money back. The cup was still pretty heavy, so I knew the chunk of ice must be pretty big. As I walked back to the store where I'd bought the slushy, I decided to lift the lid and see the enormous straw-stopper for myself. Bad move. The thing that had stopped my straw, now stopped me dead in my tracks. It wasn't a chunk of ice. What I found in the bottom of my cup seriously made me want to hurl. It was a whole, dead, squeaky-clean-because-I'd-sucked-it-that-way . . . frog! I couldn't believe it. That means every time I'd been stabbing at my chunk of ice, I'd actually been . . . ugh, I can't even write it.

Did you know that God gets disgusted the same way? Yeah, that's right. The big guy upstairs actually blows chunks. But not from finding amphibious creatures in his beverages. The thing that makes God sick is when people don't use the gifts he's given them for his glory. How can we be useful to him when we're always 'straddling the fence' between being full-on for him and doing stuff to please ourselves?

I don't know about you, but I'd rather be a useful, refreshing slushy in God's cup than a cold, dead frog.

God's mind

I know what you do, that you are neither hot nor cold. I wish that you were either hot or cold! But because you are warm – neither hot, nor cold – I am ready to spit you out of my mouth.
Revelation 3:15–16

The potter can make anything he wants to make. He can use the same clay to make one thing for special use and another thing for daily use.
Romans 9:21

God never changes his mind about the people he calls and the things he gives them.
Romans 11:29

There are different kinds of gifts, but they are all from the same Spirit. There are different ways to serve but the same Lord to serve. And there are different ways that God works through people but the same God. God works in all of us in everything we do.
I Corinthians 12:4–6

I wish that you were either **hot or cold!**

your mind

What's the most disgusting thing I've ever tasted?

What does it mean to be 'hot or cold' to God?

What does it mean to be 'lukewarm'?

Here's a list of gifts/talents God has given me:

1.

2.

3.

4.

5.

How can I use these gifts/talents for his glory?

HEALING

chipK's mind

Some people think that miraculous healings only happened back in Bible times. Hogwash! How do I know? Because I've experienced one myself.

When I was a kid, my left foot was turned in slightly. It affected the way I stood, walked, ran – everything. One night my dad sensed God's leading to pray for my foot to be healed as he tucked me into bed. I was already asleep, but as he prayed for me, my foot turned straight, and by the next morning it was obvious that I'd been completely healed. After that, I was always the fastest runner in my class at school, and I ended up going to a Performing Arts Academy after I graduated. I think it's safe to say that had it not been for that miraculous experience, I'd not be the on-stage dancing, mental lunatic that I am today.

By the next morning it was obvious that I'd been completely healed

This is just one of many stories of people being physically healed all over the world in *our* time. There are other types of healing too. Some people experience emotional healing from past hurts and abuse. Others may need healing in their minds. Everyone who becomes a follower of Jesus experiences a sort of 'spiritual' healing to some degree. We've gone from being children trapped in darkness, stuck in a prison of doing what's wrong, to being children of the Light, set free to enjoy the pleasures of God forever.

Not all supernatural healings happen instantly. Sometimes God chooses to heal us over a period of time. In some cases, God chooses to not heal people at all (not in the way they expect him to anyway). In times like these, no matter how stubborn we may be, we have to trust that he knows what he's doing.

After all, he is God isn't he?

God's mind

But he was wounded for the wrong we did; he was crushed for the evil we did. The punishment, which made us well, was given to him, and we are healed because of his wounds.
Isaiah 53:5

Jesus heard this and said to them, 'It is not the healthy people who need a doctor, but the sick. I do not come to invite good people but to invite sinners.'
Mark 2:17

When the sun went down, the people brought those who were sick to Jesus. Putting his hands on each sick person, he healed every one of them.
Luke 4:40

'Which is easier: to tell this paralysed man, "Your sins are forgiven," or to tell him, "Stand up. Take your mat and walk"? But I will prove to you that the Son of Man has authority on earth to forgive sins.' So, Jesus said to the paralysed man, 'I tell you, stand up, take your mat, and go home.' Immediately the paralysed man stood up, took his mat and walked out while everyone was watching him. The people were amazed and praised God. They said, 'We have never seen anything like this!'
Mark 2:9–12

Anyone who is sick should call the church's elders. They should pray for and pour oil on the person in the name of the Lord. And the prayer that is said with faith will make the sick person well; the Lord will heal that person. And if the person has sinned, the sins will be forgiven.
James 5:14–15

'Then if my people, who are called by my name, are sorry for what they have done, if they pray and obey me and stop their evil ways, I will hear them from heaven. I will forgive their sin, and I will heal their land.'
2 Chronicles 7:14

your mind

Is there anything I'd like to be healed from:

○ **Physically? (in my body)**
_____

○ **Mentally? (in my mind)**
_____

○ **Emotionally? (in my feelings)**_____
_____

○ **Spiritually? (in my heart)**
_____

Who can I talk to that will pray with me to find healing?

Who can I pray *for* right now to receive healing?

When it comes to healing, why is it always better to pray in groups of two or more? (HINT: Matthew 18:19–20)

GRACE OLYMPICS

chipK's mind

No doubt about it, the Chinese are amazing athletes. Need proof? Check 'em out at the Olympic Games. They have an unbelievable knack of combining strength, speed and beauty with an almost effortless flair.

Athens, Greece, 2004
The finals competition for Men's Synchronized Diving

**And then...
belly-flop**

China was ranked number one by the end of the heats, and all they needed was one more of those famous performances to clinch the gold. Just one dive left. And then . . . belly-flop. The judges' scores all came up – zero. Those two Chinese divers had gone from hero status to zero status, and all in less than a second.

The Bible encourages us to 'run the race with perseverance', comparing our lives to a competition, just like in the Olympics. But I can't help thinking that, actually, if we're really honest with ourselves, we can identify more with those two unfortunate Chinese guys than any of the hundreds of gold medallists. We belly-flop every day when we mess up and sin, yet we're still encouraged to 'press on towards the prize' of heaven. God's grace says, 'You know what? Even though you've belly-flopped, I've still got a gold medal with your name on it.'

That's something we need to hear loud and clear . . . and not just every four years.

God's mind

We have around us many people whose lives tell us what faith means. So let us run the race that is before us and never give up. We should remove from our lives anything that would get in the way and the sin that so easily holds us back. Let us look only to Jesus, the One who began our faith and who makes it perfect. He suffered death on the cross. But he accepted the shame as if it were nothing because of the joy that God put before him. And now he is sitting at the right side of God's throne. Think about Jesus' example. He held on while wicked people were doing evil things to him. So do not get tired and stop trying.
Hebrews 12:1–3

But he said to me, 'My grace is enough for you.'
2 Corinthians 12:9a

I do not mean that I am already as God wants me to be. I have not yet reached that goal, but I continue trying to reach it and to make it mine. Christ wants me to do that, which is the reason he made me his. Brothers and sisters, I know that I have not yet reached that goal, but there is one thing I always do. Forgetting the past and straining towards what is ahead, I keep trying to reach the goal and get the prize for which God called me through Christ to the life above.
Philippians 3:12–14

Also an athlete who takes part in a contest must obey all the rules in order to win.
2 Timothy 2:5

your mind

What do athletes spend most of their time doing?

How does this apply to my personal 'Grace Olympics'?

What is a simple definition of 'grace'? (HINT: Feel free to use a dictionary)

What potential 'belly-flops' can I avoid today?

UPGRADE

chipK's mind

Ilya wasn't the most popular guy in our youth group. He was a big, slightly clumsy, soft-spoken Russian kid who, if truth be told, would sometimes stink of the worst body odour you could imagine. Everyone pretty much avoided him at church, even though he made many attempts to join our little cliques. That is, until one fateful plane ride.

We were flying home from a mission trip to Slovakia. There were around twenty of us in the youth group, and we were mostly sat at the back of the plane, along with the designated chaperones (one of which was my mom, who was sat right next to me). But Ilya somehow managed to get an upgraded seat in *first class*. To this day, I still cannot work out how the biggest, sweatiest, clumsiest one of us landed himself the comfiest spot on that plane.

Shortly after we'd settled in for the long flight, my mom got up and went down to the front to check on Ilya. She'd expected to find the happiest kid alive – feet propped up and snackin' on loads of extra food. Instead, she found Ilya slouched down in his massive seat, utterly miserable. 'What's wrong, Ilya?' she asked him. 'I'm sad because I want to be with my friends,' he replied. After a short pause, Ilya asked my mom, 'Who are you sitting next to back there?' 'I'm sitting next to Chip,' she said . . . That's when the inevitable happened. They swapped seats. Let's just say, there were two very happy passengers on board for the rest of that long flight. One at the front, and one (just one) at the back.

In hindsight, I can see how childish we were to make Ilya feel like such an outsider. He was just as much a child of God as any of us were, and yet we were too selfish to treat him like one. According to the Bible, Jesus wasn't exactly the best looking, nicest smelling, most popular guy to hang around with either. He had nothing in his appearance to attract us to him. Sure, his miracles and wise words drew crowds in by the thousands, but the Bible still calls him a 'man of sorrows'. He understands what it's like to feel rejected and friendless.

Even when you're sitting in first class.

God's mind

He had no special beauty or form to make us notice him; there was nothing in his appearance to make us desire him. He was hated and rejected by people. He had much pain and suffering. People would not even look at him. He was hated, and we didn't even notice him.
Isaiah 53:2b–3

But the Lord said to Samuel, 'Don't look at how handsome Eliab is or how tall he is, because I have not chosen him. God does not see the same way people see. People look at the outside of a person, but the Lord looks at the heart.'
1 Samuel 16:7

It is not fancy hair, gold jewellery or fine clothes that should make you beautiful. No, your beauty should come from within you – the beauty of a gentle and quiet spirit that will never be destroyed and is very precious to God.
1 Peter 3:3–4

Charm can fool you, and beauty can trick you, but a woman who respects the Lord should be praised.
Proverbs 31:30

Brothers and sisters, look at what you were when God called you. Not many of you were wise in the way the world judges wisdom. Not many of you had great influence. Not many of you came from important families. But God chose the foolish things of the world to shame the wise, and he chose the weak things of the world to shame the strong. He chose what the world thinks is unimportant and what the world looks down on and thinks is nothing in order to destroy what the world thinks is important. God did this so that no one can boast in his presence.'
1 Corinthians 1:26–29

your mind

Who do I know that isn't very popular?

What makes him/her so unpopular?

What makes this person popular to God?

How can I make this person feel special today?

PEACE

chipK's mind

When God called our family to move to Israel in 1990, it was only months before Saddam Hussein began making threats of launching a chemical warfare attack – the beginnings of what would become the Gulf War (the first time round). We prayed about whether or not we should fly home to America, but we all felt God was saying we should stay put. So we did. Over a period of months, we endured twenty-three nights of air raid sirens alerting us to make our way to our 'sealed room' (surrounded by plastic) and strap on our emergency gas masks. One night we actually heard the missiles exploding over our house!

God gave us a supernatural peace

While all this was going on, we really should have been shaking in our boots, afraid of what might happen next. Instead, God gave us a supernatural peace that didn't make any sense. Even though sometimes we were stuck in that sealed room for what seemed like an eternity, we were all pretty chilled out. In fact, after a while, it actually got quite annoying, especially when the siren would start up just as we were sitting down to dinner. My mom would shake her fist at Saddam for ruining her perfectly warm meal.

When the disciples were faced with a life-threatening storm out on the Sea of Galilee, they were absolutely brickin' it. And where was Jesus? Asleep, down below deck. What did he say to the storm when they freaked out and woke him up? 'Peace, be still.'

When we're worried, stressed, afraid and uncertain, that's when we need to know God's peace the most. And that's when it's most available.

God's mind

You, Lord, give true peace to those who depend on you, because they trust you.
Isaiah 26:3

'I leave you peace; my peace I give you. I do not give it to you as the world does. So don't let your hearts be troubled or afraid.'
John 14:27

Let the peace that Christ gives control your thinking, because you were all called together in one body to have peace.
Colossians 3:15a

Jesus got into a boat, and his followers went with him. A great storm arose on the lake so that waves covered the boat, but Jesus was sleeping. His followers went to him and woke him, saying, 'Lord, save us! We will drown!' Jesus answered, 'Why are you afraid? You don't have enough faith.' Then Jesus got up and gave a command to the wind and the waves, and it became completely calm. The men were amazed and said, 'What kind of man is this? Even the wind and the waves obey him!'
Matthew 8:23–27

Do not worry about anything, but pray and ask God for everything you need, always giving thanks. And God's peace, which is so great we cannot understand it, will keep your hearts and minds in Christ Jesus.
Philippians 4:6–7

'Those who work to bring peace are happy, because God will call them his children.'
Matthew 5:9

your mind

What's the most un-peaceful situation I've ever been in?

Why is it always better to be peaceful rather than stressful?

Who do I know who is always peaceful?

How can I be a peace*maker* today?

When am I most at peace?

TRUST-MUSCLE

chipK's mind

Everyday, all the time, people are exercising what I like to call their 'trust-muscle'. Everybody has one, but not everyone uses it for the same things. Now don't get me wrong. There are some things that everyone uses their trust-muscles for. Take for instance, gravity. We all trust that the earth's gravitational pull will continue to keep us from randomly flying off into outer space. Otherwise, we'd be walking around with massive lead weights attached to our ankles.

When everyone else lets you down, he won't

Another example – door locks. Especially in the loo. When the bathroom door is locked, we find tremendous security in the fact that no one can walk in on us. However, when the door *isn't* locked or the lock isn't functioning properly, our trust-muscles start working overtime. I'm sure you've experienced something like this before: You're sat there with your trousers around your ankles, and you hear someone approaching your cubicle. Just as they're about to try your door, a thought suddenly enters your mind . . . 'I haven't locked it'. That's when everything turns into slow motion, a bit like bullet-time in the Matrix movies, only with much more embarrassing kind of special effects. Your hand reaches out to keep the door shut, but it's too late . . . and there's nothing you can do about it.

There are other things which we aren't very used to exercising our trust-muscles for. Like other people. Take, for instance, politicians or ex-boyfriends/girlfriends or even well meaning parents. This is usually because we feel that they've let us down in the past, or they haven't proved themselves to be very trust*worthy*.

Jesus promised that he would be with us always – even to the end of the world. When everyone else lets you down, he won't. There may be times when you think he has, but he hasn't.

He's just exercising your trust-muscle.

God's mind

'I will be with you always, even until the end of this age.'
Matthew 28:20b

Just as I was with Moses, so I will be with you. I will not leave you or forget you.
Joshua 1:5b

Trust the Lord with all your heart, and don't depend on your own understanding. Remember the Lord in all you do, and he will give you success.
Proverbs 3:5–6

But Jesus paid no attention to what they said. He told the synagogue leader, 'Don't be afraid; just believe.'
Mark 5:36

People, trust God all the time. Tell him all your problems, because God is our protection.
Psalm 62:8

Trust the Lord with all your heart, and don't depend on your own understanding

your mind

Who/what do I exercise my trust-muscle for all the time?

Who/what have I found to be extremely *untrustworthy*?

Why is God the best person to put all my trust in?

What are three things I've been given that God actually trusts me with?

1.

2.

3.

TITHES and OFFERINGS

chipK's mind

He wants us to give cheerfully, knowing that his love comes free of charge

All through the Bible, we find the people of God doing something slightly peculiar with their money. No matter how much or how little they earned, they would always give part of it back to God. The 'money' they gave him wasn't dollars and cents (duh), but it still meant just as much to them back then as our currency means to us today – usually a lamb or a goat or even a dove. It was called their tithes and offerings, and this is still practised by Christians today. All my life, I've always given ten per cent of the money I've earned to my church as a tithe, and any money I've given on top of that was considered my 'offering'. Even when I was receiving just one dollar a week as my allowance, I would still faithfully give ten cents back to God, plus a small offering. It was a principle which my parents considered to be extremely important and it's stuck with me ever since.

Some people argue that it's not right to tithe, and God won't love you any less if you don't – and they're absolutely correct. If the only reason we're giving our tithes and offerings is because we feel obliged to, then God would rather that we didn't give at all. He wants us to give cheerfully, knowing that his love comes free of charge.

If it helps, think of it like this: tithing is giving back to God what's already his. Offerings are gifts given in faith to the Giver of all we have. That's a lot of giving!

God's mind

Each one should give as he has decided in his heart to give. You should not be sad when you give, and you should not give because you feel forced to give. God loves the person who gives happily.
2 Corinthians 9:7

'Give, and you will receive. You will be given much. Pressed down, shaken together and running over, it will spill into your lap. The way you give to others is the way God will give to you.'
Luke 6:38

As soon as the king's command went out to the Israelites, they gave freely of the first portion of their grain, new wine, oil, honey and everything they grew in their fields. They brought a large amount, one-tenth of everything.
2 Chronicles 31:5

Give an offering to show thanks to God. Give God Most High what you have promised.
Psalm 50:14

I taught you to remember the words Jesus said: 'It is more blessed to give than to receive.'
Acts 20: 35b

Give, and you will receive. You will be given much

your mind

Why is money so valuable to us?

Do tithes and offerings always have to be given in the form of money?

How faithfully do I tithe?

Why is it better to give than to get?

I will commit to giving God my tithes and offerings from the money I've earned by:

CREATION

chipK's mind

A few years ago, Helen and I had the amazing opportunity of spending six weeks in New Zealand. Most of the time we were working, but shortly before we left we had about a week to check out some of the breathtaking scenery this island nation has to offer. One such stop off was at a place right next to the big mountain you'll see at the start of every Paramount film – it's called Fox's Glacier. We felt like Arctic explorers as we slowly and carefully trekked up the icy glacier, stopping only to top our water bottles up with the freshest, cleanest, most freezing cold water we'd ever tasted, from tiny babbling waterfalls along the way. We also went to Lake Mattheson where we took pictures from a spot called the 'Holy of Holies'. It was, undoubtedly, the single most beautiful landscape view I'd ever seen. When our photographs were developed, they simply paled in comparison to seeing the majesty of God's creation firsthand.

We felt like Arctic explorers as we trekked up the icy glacier

When God created the earth, he hid little clues about himself everywhere. The gentle beauty of an ocean sunset, the fury of a volcanic eruption, even the slow, steady flowing of a mighty ancient glacier . . . These are all characteristics of the Creator himself.

It's up to us to discover them for ourselves.

God's mind

Yes, God has shown himself to them. There are things about him that people cannot see – his eternal power and all the things that make him God. But since the beginning of the world those things have been easy to understand by what God has made. So people have no excuse for the bad things they do.
Romans 1:19b–20

The heavens tell the glory of God and the skies announce what his hands have made. Day after day they tell the story; night after night they tell it again. They have no speech or words; they have no voice to be heard. But their message goes out through all the world; their words go everywhere on earth.
Psalm 19:1–4

Go and watch the ants, you lazy person. Watch what they do and be wise.
Proverbs 6:6

The heavens tell the **glory of God** and the skies announce what **his hands** have made

your mind

What is the most beautiful natural view/sight I've ever seen?

Why did God take the time to 'hide' his characteristics in his creation instead of just telling plainly?

What can I learn about God by studying these examples from nature:

A tree:

A sunset:

An African lion:

A snowflake:

A mountain:

A waterfall:

A slug:

I will take time to stop and consider God's attributes in his creation by:

61

PURITY

chipK's mind

'What do you think it means to be *pure*?' The question was being asked by the leader of an after school club that I visit as often as I can. My young friend confidently raised his hand. 'Orange juice', he said. Hmm. Not quite the answer I was expecting, and I'm not entirely sure it was the answer our club leader was fishing for. But I can see the connection.

To most Christian young people, being *pure* means not having sex with someone until after you're married to them. By abstaining from all sexual behaviour before marriage, you are respecting your future husband or wife and keeping your body pure for them. This totally goes against the current trend of showing someone you 'really love them' by losing your virginity to them without waiting and marrying them first. The Bible calls this 'fornication', and you know what? It's not something you want to mess around with. It's not the way God designed us to behave. The consequences are huge – unwanted pregnancies, abortion, sexually transmitted diseases and so on. Even so-called 'safe sex' is always extremely dangerous when it's outside of God's perfect plan. You've still got to face the consequences of guilt, emotional scars and ungodly relationships which are difficult to abandon.

I kept my virginity right up to my wedding night. You can too. God wants us to save ourselves for our future spouse, no matter how unpopular it may seem at the time. Sex is totally part of God's plan for us, and he knows that it is most enjoyable when it's kept within the boundaries of marriage. Once they've 'tied the knot', it is a truly beautiful thing for two virgins to explore the furthest regions of their love for each other through sex. They're able to fully trust each other because of the commitment they've made. They've got the rest of their lives ahead of them to drink deeply of love.

And this is a love that is pure – just like orange juice.

God's mind

But run away from the evil young people like to do. Try hard to live right and to have faith, love and peace, together with those who trust in the Lord from pure hearts.
2 Timothy 2:22

So run away from sexual sin. Every other sin people do is outside their bodies, but those who sin sexually sin against their own bodies. You should know that your body is a temple for the Holy Spirit who is in you. You have received the Holy Spirit from God. So you do not belong to yourselves, because you were bought by God for a price. So honour God with your bodies.
1 Corinthians 6:18–20

But there must be no sexual sin among you, or any kind of evil or greed. Those things are not right for God's holy people.
Ephesians 5:3

How can a young person live a pure life? By obeying your word.
Psalm 119:9

God called us to be holy and does not want us to live in sin.
1 Thessalonians 4:7

'Those who are pure in their thinking are happy, because they will be with God.'
Matthew 5:8

your mind

What are the benefits of sleeping around and experimenting with sex outside of marriage?

And the consequences? (Try to be more specific than the list already provided)

Is my body even mine to give away in the first place?

If not, then whose is it?

Okay, so I'm not going to have sex before marriage. How far should I go with my boyfriend/girlfriend? (HINT: You might want to get some advice from an older, more experienced Christian on this one.)

63

FORGIVENESS

The Mind of chipK

chipK's mind

Most of the time, my sister and I get along just fine. But when we were younger we used to get into some terrible fights. I would call her names (my favourite was 'fat-hog-slog-pig'. Isn't that a great one? . . . um . . . I mean . . .. Isn't that terrible?), and she would respond by launching into a full-on physical assault. She knew I wasn't allowed to hit girls back, so that was always her weapon of choice. One of our parents would inevitably break up the fight, telling us to apologize and forgive each other. Isn't it amazing how the words 'I forgive you' can be spoken through gritted teeth and squinted eyes, yet still sound totally convincing?

God's love for us is unconditional. His anger towards our sin was completely used up on Jesus when he died in our place. When we admit the wrong stuff we've done and tell God how sorry we truly are, he will always forgive us. He chucks our sin as far away from us as the east is from the west. That's pretty far.

God's love for us is unconditional

No matter how badly you've messed up, it's never too late to repent and ask God to forgive you.

He's a gracious Father who specializes in second-chance-giving, and his arms of love are wide open.

God's mind

Then Peter came to Jesus and asked, 'Lord, when my fellow believer sins against me, how many times must I forgive him? Should I forgive him as many as seven times?' Jesus answered, 'I tell you, you must forgive him more than seven times. You must forgive him even if he does wrong to you 77 times.'
Matthew 18:21–22

'When you are praying, if you are angry with someone, forgive him so that your Father in heaven will also forgive your sins.'
Mark 11:25

If we say we have no sin, we are fooling ourselves, and the truth is not in us. But if we confess our sins, he will forgive our sins, because we can trust God to do what is right. He will cleanse us from all the wrongs we have done.
1 John 1:8–9

He has taken our sins away from us as far as the east is from the west.
Psalm 103:12

His anger lasts only a moment, but his kindness lasts for a lifetime. Crying may last for a night, but joy comes in the morning.
Psalm 30:5

If we **confess** our sins, he will **forgive** our sins

your mind

The last section dealt with sexual sin. Can God even forgive that?

Why is it never easy to ask someone to forgive me?

If someone who's offended me badly comes asking for forgiveness, why should I forgive them?

Do I need to seek forgiveness today from God or anyone else? If so, who? And what for?

BULLET-PROOF VEST

chipK's mind

I used to have a recurring dream where I'd show up for school wearing only my underwear. Somehow I'd been in such a rush to get there on time that I'd managed to forget to put any clothes on. I was forced to endure the stares and laughter of all my friends for the remainder of my embarrassing school day. Of course, the best part was waking up, relieved that it was only a bad dream!

Spiritually speaking, I'm sad to say that a lot of Christians really do walk around wearing only their 'underwear'. You can find them not only in schools, but also in places of work, at home, in cinemas, in the gym and even in churches. They're the ones who've forgotten to put their spiritual *armour* on.

The Bible lists some of these key pieces of armour (Ephesians 6):

- Belt of truth
- Bullet-proof vest of righteousness
- Boots of Good News of peace
- Shield of faith
- Helmet of salvation
- Sword of the Spirit (God's Word)

This armour protects us from the tricks, schemes and temptations the devil throws our way. Each one of them is just as important as the other in fighting the spiritual battles we face every day. Take time to put them on spiritually, mentally, and even physically if you have to.

After all, you don't want the embarrassment of showing up in your underwear, do you?

God's mind

Finally, be strong in the Lord and in his great power. Put on the full armour of God so that you can fight against the devil's evil tricks. Our fight is not against people on earth but against the rulers and authorities and the powers of this world's darkness, against the spiritual powers of evil in the heavenly world. That is why you need to put on God's full armour. Then on the day of evil you will be able to stand strong. And when you have finished the whole fight, you will still be standing. So stand strong, with the belt of truth tied around your waist and the protection of right living on your chest. On your feet wear the Good News of peace to help you stand strong. And also use the shield of faith with which you can stop all the burning arrows of the Evil One. Accept God's salvation as your helmet, and take the sword of the Spirit, which is the word of God.'
Ephesians 6:10–17

Fight the good fight of faith, grabbing hold of the life that continues forever.
1 Timothy 6:12a

Share in the troubles we have like a good soldier of Christ Jesus. A soldier wants to please the enlisting officer so no one serving in the army wastes time with everyday matters.
2 Timothy 2:3–4

The 'night' is almost finished, and the 'day' is almost here. So we should stop doing things that belong to darkness and take up the weapons used for fighting in the light. . . . But clothe yourselves with the Lord Jesus Christ and forget about satisfying your sinful self.
Romans 13:12,14

He covered himself with goodness like armour. He put the helmet of salvation on his head. He put on the clothes of punishment and wrapped himself in the coat of his strong love.
Isaiah 59:17

your mind

Take time to study this list of body armour. What else have I learned about each of these?

○ **Truth:**

○ **Righteousness:**

○ **Peace (HINT: Isaiah 52:7; Romans 10:14–15):**

○ **Faith:**

○ **Salvation:**

○ **God's Word:**

At what point today is my spiritual armour most likely to be tested?

BULLET-PROOF VEST

The Mind of chipK

GOD'S WORD

chipK's mind

My friend Zulu is incredible. He's like a walking, talking, living, breathing Bible. Seriously, I've never known anyone who can quote so much of the scripture all the time as part of his daily life. Get this, he's even recorded himself rapping the book of Revelation, and plans on seeing the other sixty-five books of the Bible recorded by other rappers as well!

Search the Bible as if digging for hidden treasure

Zulu is seriously passionate about God's word. And why shouldn't he be? The Bible continues to be the best-selling book of all time. It was inspired by God's Spirit thousands of years ago and, even still, no one can add to its profound truth. King Solomon, the wisest man who ever lived, wrote a few of its chapters, telling us to search the Bible as if we were digging for hidden treasure. And it's not just because it's a good book. Remember how the 'precious' ring from *The Lord of the Rings* trilogy would grow and shrink to fit the finger of its wearer? Well, in the same way, the Word of God is alive and active, revealing different things to different people at just the right time. On top of that, it's compared to being like the sharpest sword ever, full of power to cut deep into our secret thoughts and desires, exposing us for what we really are. No matter what difficult situation you're experiencing, no matter how many times you've done it before, you can always turn to the Bible for the best advice around.

Now please excuse me while I go bust some rhymes from Leviticus.

God's mind

Your word is like a lamp for my feet and a light for my path.
Psalm 119:105

God's word is alive and working and is sharper than a double-edged sword. It cuts all the way into us, where the soul and the spirit are joined, to the centre of our joints and bones. And it judges the thoughts and feelings in our hearts.
Hebrews 4:12

Cry out for wisdom, and beg for understanding. Search for it like silver, and hunt for it like hidden treasure.
Proverbs 2:3–4

I have taken your words to heart so I would not sin against you. Lord, you should be praised. Teach me your demands. My lips will tell about all the laws you have spoken. I enjoy living by your rules as people enjoy great riches. I think about your orders and study your ways. I enjoy obeying your demands, and I will not forget your word. Do good to me, your servant, so I can live, so I can obey your word. Open my eyes to see the miracles in your teachings. I am a stranger on earth. Do not hide your commands from me.
Psalm 119:11–19

All Scripture is given by God and is useful for teaching, for showing people what is wrong in their lives, for correcting faults and for teaching how to live right. Using the Scriptures, the person who serves God will be capable, having all that is needed to do every good work.
2 Timothy 3: 16–17

your mind

GOD'S WORD

Who wrote the Bible?

What is my favourite Scripture?

Why is it so important not only to read the Bible, but to memorize it?

How often *can* I read the Bible?

How often *do* I read the Bible?

How often *will* I read the Bible from now on?

69

SCHIZOPHRENIC SKIN

chipK's mind

You've been sentenced to live in an empty padded cell. The straightjacket you're wearing keeps your arms strapped to your body so you can't move them. The only light in your room comes from a single flickering bulb and, just like that bulb, you're all alone.

Or so you think.

No one enters your cell, but a voice enters your head. Then another one joins in. And another. These voices in your head continue to grow louder and louder until your only option is to lose your self . . . and become one of them.

There is only one doctor who can save us from ourselves

[cue the evil laughter]

Okay, so maybe this is a slightly over-the-top Hollywood version of what it means to be a schizophrenic. But actually I believe that every human being on the planet suffers from a slight variation of this horrific mental disorder. The Bible calls it 'sin'. It's the stuff we do every day that displeases God and goes against the way he designed us to be. One moment we're walking along quite happy and content through a shopping mall, and the next we're drooling outside a shop window, coveting some ridiculously expensive piece of clothing. It's like we've got a split personality. One side wants to be holy and do things right, the other side will lie, steal, cheat and do anything else it can to get what it wants. The apostle Paul wrote all about this struggle with sin (Romans 7). He comes to the conclusion that there is only one doctor who can save us from ourselves. The cure starts when we make him our Master.

I think you know *who* I'm talking about.

God's mind

We know that the law is spiritual, but I am not spiritual since sin rules me as if I were its slave. I do not understand the things I do. I do not do what I want to do, and I do the things I hate. And if I do not want to do the hated things I do, that means I agree that the law is good. But I am not really the one who is doing these hated things; it is sin living in me that does them. Yes, I know that nothing good lives in me – I mean nothing good lives in the part of me that is earthly and sinful. I want to do the things that are good, but I do not do them. . . . So if I do things I do not want to do, then I am not the one doing them. It is sin living in me that does those things. So I have learned this rule: when I want to do good, evil is there with me. In my mind, I am happy with God's law. But I see another law working in my body, which makes war against the law that my mind accepts. That other law working in my body is the law of sin, and it makes me its prisoner. What a miserable man I am! Who will save me from this body that brings me death? I thank God for saving me through Jesus Christ our Lord!'
Romans 7:14–25a

All have sinned and are not good enough for God's glory, and all need to be made right with God by his grace, which is a free gift. They need to be made free from sin through Jesus Christ.
Romans 3:23–24

Christ had no sin, but God made him become sin so that in Christ we could become right with God.
2 Corinthians 5:21

So I tell you: live by following the Spirit. Then you will not do what your sinful selves want. Our sinful selves want what is against the Spirit, and the Spirit wants what is against our sinful selves. The two are against each other, so you cannot do just what you please.
Galatians 5:16–17

Those who belong to Christ Jesus have crucified their own sinful selves. They have given up their old selfish feelings and the evil things they wanted to do.
Galatians 5:24

your mind

What sins do I struggle with the most? (HINT: Be honest!)

Why are these sins bad? How are they contrary to God's perfect plan, and what are the consequences of doing them?

Why is Jesus the only person who can start to cure me of my schizophrenic skin? What has he done that's so important?

When will I be fully cured?

H.S.

chipK's mind

Maureen was the craziest woman I'd ever met. Maureen was by far the most unorthodox, untamed and unusual individual I'd ever laid eyes on. Maureen was my *ballet teacher*.

I'll never forget the way she used to pout her big lips whenever she'd catch one of her terrified pupils 'turning out' (standing with your heels together) incorrectly from their knees. 'Inner thighs!' she'd shout. 'Inner thighs! I wanna see mashed potatoes and gravy!' (whatever that means!) Then she'd spend the rest of the afternoon on top of a ladder in the corner of the room, watching us like a hawk about to devour its prey.

Despite all of her strange antics, though, Maureen did teach us all an extremely important truth, right in the middle of one of her famous ballet classes. She stopped everything and marched up to the chalkboard. 'What is the most important thing in the world?' she asked, as she picked up a piece of chalk. Some brave soul shouted out 'Dance!' and she wrote it on the board. Someone else shouted 'Love!' so she wrote that on the board as well. On and on, everyone took turns calling out their philosophies on the meaning of life, and she patiently wrote it on the board, shaking her head as if to say we still weren't getting it right. At one point, a few of us desperately cried, 'Inner thighs?!' hoping *that* was the correct answer. Finally, Maureen drew a massive circle around everything she'd written and said, 'These are all great answers, but what do they *all* have in common?' We just stood there, not knowing what else to say. She decided to give us the answer herself. 'The most important thing in the world is . . . the Holy Spirit.' She said it slowly as she wrote it in massive letters across the entire board. Oh!

Maureen wasn't entirely off her rocker, you know. As time went on, I began to discover how important the Holy Spirit really is. He's not a thing; he's actually a person with a mind (thoughts), a will (purpose) and emotions (feelings). He's the one who inspired all the prophets, kings and scribes to write the entire Bible (2 Peter 1:20–21). He's our counsellor (John 14:16–18), our gift-giver (1 Corinthians 12:4–11) and the one who develops good fruit in our lives (Galatians 5:22–23).

If you haven't already, I'd encourage you to do a study on H.S. for yourself. Here's a ton of Scriptures to get you started. And I promise, none of them talk about your inner thighs.

God's mind

your mind

We get our new life from the Spirit, so we should follow the Spirit.
Galatians 5:25

The earth was empty and had no form. Darkness covered the ocean, and God's Spirit was moving over the water.
Genesis 1:2

Then the Lord said to Moses, 'See, I have chosen Bezalel, son of Uri, from the tribe of Judah. (Uri was the son of Hur.) I have filled Bezalel with the Spirit of God and have given him the skill, ability and knowledge to do all kinds of work. He is able to design pieces to be made from gold, silver and bronze, to cut jewels and put them in metal, to carve wood, and to do all kinds of work.
Exodus 31:1–5

Judges 6:14–16

Judges 15:14–15

Isaiah 61:1–3

Luke 1:15

Luke 1:35

Luke 1:67

Luke 2:25–27

Luke 3:21–22

Acts 2:3

What have I learned about H.S. that I didn't know before?

**Why is it so important to treat H.S. as a *person* rather than a power or a force?
(HINT: Acts 8:9–24)**

When in my life have I experienced H.S. functioning as my counsellor?

What is the 'most important thing in the world'?

IDENTITY

chipK's mind

CASE ONE: A CASE OF MISTAKEN IDENTITY
My family was always one of the last to leave church after the Sunday service was over. For my sister and me, these often proved to be difficult times, waiting around while our grown-up parents stood there speaking in their grown-up language to other grown-ups. How thoroughly boring. All we wanted to do was go home. Once, out of pure desperation, I ran up to my mom, let out a massive sigh and threw my arms around her waist. 'Hello there, Chip.' It wasn't my mother's voice. It wasn't my mother! I'd just desperately thrown my arms around the waist of the lady who lived next door to us. I slowly walked away to the sound of her grown-up friends' laughter. As my cheeks turned red, she very sweetly called out, 'I love you too!'

Many people find their own identity in the things people say about them. 'This is Susie, she's a dancer,' or 'This is Robert, and he's rubbish at cooking.' Others find their identity from what the media says about their *kind.* That's why there are so many different magazines out there, offering advice and opinions to whatever *kind* of people they're targeting. Still others find their identity in the things they love to do. Ever heard the phrase, 'You are what you eat', or 'You are what you worship'? Some people are absolutely mad about shopping; others can't seem to get enough of sport. Their identity is wrapped up in whatever they give most of their time to.

CASE TWO: A CASE OF TRUE IDENTITY
When we begin to look at the Bible, we find that God has an entirely different identity for us than what the world tries to offer. We start to understand that, actually, we're citizens of heaven, only visiting this planet for a brief vapour of time.

As you read God's Word today, take time to concentrate on what he says about you. That's your true identity.

God's mind

But you are a chosen people, royal priests, a holy nation, a people for God's own possession. You were chosen to tell about the wonderful acts of God, who called you out of darkness into his wonderful light. At one time you were not a people, but now you are God's people. In the past you had never received mercy, but now you have received God's mercy. Dear friends, you are like foreigners and strangers in this world. I beg you to avoid the evil . . .'
1 Peter 2:9–11a

Think only about the things in heaven, not the things on earth. Your old sinful self has died, and your new life is kept with Christ in God. Christ is our life, and when he comes again, you will share in his glory.
Colossians 3:2–4

But our homeland is in heaven, and we are waiting for our Saviour, the Lord Jesus Christ, to come from heaven. By his power to rule all things, he will change our simple bodies and make them like his own glorious body.
Philippians 3:20–21

Then you will be innocent and without any wrong. You will be God's children without fault. But you are living with crooked and evil people all around you, among whom you shine like stars in the dark world.
Philippians 2:15

your mind

When was the last time I experienced a case of mistaken identity?

How would my best friend describe me?

Which activities do I most identify with?

What have I learned from the Bible that God says about *me*?

Festival:Manchester, summer 2003
30,000 people having 'church' in the park

I'm a guy, man! me and presha on stage in Norway

goofing off with bobsta
before going on stage at F:M

Zulu prays a lot

FASTING

chipK's mind

I have a sort of special relationship with Kellogg's Crunchy Nut Red. Anyone who knows me well knows that I'm an obsessed lover of the stuff. I used it to illustrate a point once while preaching in a local church, and I found out afterwards that one of its inventors was right there in the congregation. I suppose it's a good thing I mentioned how much I *enjoyed* eating it!

> 'God, I'd rather hear from you than eat'

There are times (difficult times, I assure you), however, when I must refrain from eating, not just my beloved Crunchy Nut Red, but every kind of food, altogether. Instead, I spend the time I would normally spend eating, praying and reading the Bible. It's called 'fasting'. Whenever I'm in a situation where I desperately need to hear God's voice or see him accomplish something in my life, fasting is my way of saying, 'God, I'd rather hear from you than eat.'

People in the Bible did it all the time. Whenever the big prophet dude called a holy fast, the entire nation would spend a whole day just sitting there listening to him read from the Scriptures. Moses fasted when he went up on the mountain to talk to God and get the Ten Commandments. Jesus fasted for forty whole days while he was tested in the wilderness. He went on to teach his disciples, saying, '*When* you fast . . .' not '*If* you fast'. That means it's something everyone who's serious about being a follower of Jesus can and should do.

And once you've finished, I've got the ultimate 'break-fast' cereal . . .

God's mind

'When you give up eating, don't put on a sad face like the hypocrites. They make their faces look sad to show people they are giving up eating. I tell you the truth, those hypocrites already have their full reward. So when you give up eating, comb your hair and wash your face. Then people will not know that you are giving up eating, but your Father, whom you cannot see, will see you. Your Father sees what is done in secret, and he will reward you.'
Matthew 6:16–17

'This kind of special day is not what I want. This is not the way I want people to be sorry for what they have done. I don't want people just to bow their heads like a plant and wear rough cloth and lie in ashes to show their sadness. This is what you do on your special days when you do not eat, but do you think this is what the Lord wants? I will tell you the kind of special day I want: free the people you have put in prison unfairly and undo their chains. Free those to whom you are unfair and stop their hard labour. Share your food with the hungry and bring poor, homeless people into your own homes. When you see someone who has no clothes, give him yours, and don't refuse to help your own relatives.'
Isaiah 58:5–7

Moses stayed there with the Lord 40 days and 40 nights, and during that time he did not eat food or drink water. And Moses wrote the words of the Agreement – the Ten Commandments – on the stone tablets.
Exodus 34:28

Jesus ate nothing for 40 days and nights. After this, he was very hungry.
Matthew 4:2

your mind

Why should I consider fasting?

What else can I fast from besides food?

Why is it best to fast in secret? (HINT: Matthew 5:17)

When is the next time I will fast?

79

ACTION

chipK's mind

Have you ever been so annoyed, disturbed and upset by a certain situation that you just *had* to do something about it? It's called being 'provoked' to *action*. One example might be getting up in the middle of the night to turn off a dripping tap that's keeping you awake. Another might be giving money to a charity after feeling sorry for some starving children you've seen on television. Still another might be even more drastic, like dedicating your life to finding the cure for cancer after watching a loved one battle with the dreadful disease.

I was provoked to action after a certain visit to Manchester's very own shopping paradise, The Trafford Centre. It was a school holiday and I'd heard there was a pop band performing in the food court, so I found my way there and manoeuvred myself through the packed crowd as close to the front as I could get. As it turned out, the band was only fronting a famous modelling company, and they were touring various shopping centres telling young girls how to stay healthy and look pretty. Fair enough. But then they did something that shook me to the very core. They got five young girls onstage and offered a prize to the one who could best mimic the extremely over-the-top sexual dance moves from a music video featuring prostitutes. When those vulnerable, innocent girls proceeded to copy the filth, move for move, in front of a public crowd of all ages, I just wanted to scream, 'No!' at the top of my lungs. Instead, I went straight to the information desk and filed a formal complaint. But it wasn't enough. That day, I decided that the vision of Innervation, (setting up bands like thebandwithnoname all over the country promoting the gospel and Christian values) was no longer just a good idea. It's an absolute necessity.

Take a few extra minutes to pray and think about what provokes you. Could God be calling you to do something about it?

God's mind

In the Temple he found people selling cattle, sheep and doves. He saw others sitting at tables, exchanging different kinds of money. Jesus made a whip out of cords and forced all of them, both the sheep and cattle, to leave the Temple. He turned over the tables and scattered the money of those who were exchanging it. Then he said to those who were selling pigeons, 'Take these things out of here! Don't make my Father's house a place for buying and selling!' When this happened, the followers remembered what was written in the Scriptures: 'My strong love for your Temple completely controls me.'
John 2:14–17

Just as a person's body that does not have a spirit is dead, so faith that does nothing is dead!
James 2:26

Use every chance you have for doing good, because these are evil times.
Ephesians 5:16

Remember this! In the last days there will be many troubles, because people will love themselves, love money, boast and be proud. They will say evil things against others and will not obey their parents or be thankful or be the kind of people God wants. They will not love others, will refuse to forgive, will gossip and will not control themselves. They will be cruel, will hate what is good, will turn against their friends and will do foolish things without thinking. They will be conceited, will love pleasure instead of God, and will act as if they serve God but will not have his power. Stay away from these people.
2 Timothy 3:1–5

your mind

What provokes me to action?

Why does this affect me so much?

Who do I know who's dedicated their life to solving something that provokes them?

What is the biggest problem on earth today?

How can I help solve it?

WORSHIP

chipK's mind

If you were to ask me who my favourite Bible character is (apart from Jesus), I'd have to say David. He was described as, 'a man after God's own heart', anointed to do everything he attempted to accomplish. He killed giants in battle, married a princess, became a King himself, brought God's presence back to town and left behind a legacy of royalty including the wisest man who ever lived and eventually the Messiah (Wow!) That's what I call a role model.

David's passion was to worship God, whether he felt like it or not

But probably David's most famous quality is that he was a true worshipper. He praised God on his harp during his humble beginnings as a lonely shepherd boy out in the fields with his father's sheep. He wrote loads of Psalms, documenting his escapes from Saul (his jealous, bloodthirsty predecessor), his victories in battle, and even his not-so-honourable moments (like needing to repent after sleeping with another man's wife). Eventually he set up a big tent where loads of musicians and worshippers could praise God at any time of the day or night. David's passion was to worship God, whether he felt like it or not.

This should be the same for us today. A lot of the praise and worship songs we sing these days are positive and upbeat, and that's great. But really we should just as easily be able to come before God and honestly say, 'You know what? I've really screwed up this week and I'm not even feeling very sorry about it right now either.' Jesus said that we should worship in spirit and in truth. When we start to open up and be honest with God, he can start to lovingly change us into the image of his perfect son.

Like David, we too can be people after God's own heart.

God's mind

'The time is coming when the true worshippers will worship the Father in spirit and truth, and that time is here already. You see, the Father too is actively seeking such people to worship him. God is spirit and those who worship him must worship in spirit and truth.'
John 4:23–24

So brothers and sisters, since God has shown us great mercy, I beg you to offer your lives as a living sacrifice to him. Your offering must be only for God and pleasing to him, which is the spiritual way for you to worship.
Romans 12:1

The Lord has looked for the kind of man he wants. He has appointed him to rule his people, because you haven't obeyed his command.
1 Samuel 13:14b

I will praise the Lord at all times; his praise is always on my lips.
Psalm 34:1

Here are a few examples of brutally honest praise and worship:

Lord, why are you so far away? Why do you hide when there is trouble? Proudly, the wicked chase down those who suffer. Let them be caught in their own traps.
Psalm 10:1–2

God, I wish you would kill the wicked! Get away from me you murderers! . . . I feel only hate for them; they are my enemies.
Psalm 139:19,22

your mind

Who is my favourite Bible character?

What's my favourite worship song?

Which style of worship does God love best?

- O **Rock**
- O **Classical**
- O **Hip-hop**
- O **Drum 'n' bass**
- O **Country**
- O **Jazz**
- O **R & B**
- O **Metal**
- O **Other:**

Why is it better to be honest than just sing nice songs?

MAXIMUM LIFE

chipK's mind

I've never really been one for doing things by halves. For me, it's always been 'all or nothing'. Unfortunately (for my scalp, anyway) this also applies to my hair. Name any colour, length or style and chances are, my reply will be, 'Been there, done that.' At this precise moment it's 'albino white', but I'm already planning on turning it 'heaven blue' in time for our next big gig this Friday night! There is no doubt about it, every hair on my head is reaching its maximum potential – with no cheesy shampoo ad necessary.

We too can life life to the max

I believe that God intended us to enjoy life to its maximum potential. Especially when I look at the lifestyles of some of the people in the Bible. Check out Adam and Eve in the Garden of Eden. How cool was that? They were quite literally one with nature. That garden was perfection. And the only thing that *could* screw it all up *did* screw it all up. A human being. One wrong decision and *whabam!* The human race has to wait thousands of years for Jesus to come along and make things right again. And thank God, He did.

This means that we too – through Jesus – can have life to the max. When we do things God's way we can learn how to have fun from the inventor of fun itself. Sound like fun to you?

Now, put down that hair dye . . .

God's mind

'A thief comes to steal and kill and destroy, but I came to give life – life in all its fullness.'
John 10:10

'And this is eternal life: that people know you, the only true God, and that they know Jesus Christ, the One you sent.'
John 17:3

One man sinned, and so death ruled all people because of that one man. But now those people who accept God's full grace and the great gift of being made right with him will surely have true life and rule through the one man, Jesus Christ.
Romans 5:17

I came to **give** **life** – life in all its fullness

your mind

My perfect day would involve:

Three things that stop me from having life to the max are:

1.

2.

3.

In what ways can I experience eternal life (heaven) on earth today?

Who do I know that seems to really be enjoying a maximum life?

HUMILITY

chipK's mind

When my family travelled around, performing and ministering in churches all over the world, I would almost always do a mime/dance piece as part of the presentation. To this day, I can remember one such performance at a small church in Florida. The centrepiece of the sanctuary was a beautifully crafted glass vase in the middle of the communion table, just in front of the stage. At the end of my song I would always surprise the audience by jumping off the stage and running through the aisles, so I had to quickly size up whether or not I'd be able to clearly jump over this ornate, precious vase. In the split-second before I jumped, I thought, 'No problem, I'll clear it' . . . I didn't clear it. To my utter pain and embarrassment, my foot caught the edge of the fragile vase and it shattered into a million pieces all over the floor. That had to be the most humiliating moment of my life. And I still had to finish the performance!

Humble yourself or be humiliated. The choice is yours

When it comes to humility, my advice is this: 'Humble yourself, or be humiliated.' The choice is yours. Pride is something God hates, because it doesn't leave room for him to do what he wants to do in us. It just holds him back. Remember, pride is what ultimately got Lucifer (the devil) fired from his top position as worship leader in heaven (Isaiah 14:12–15).

Don't 'fall' for the same mistake.

God's mind

But God gives us even more grace, as the scripture says, 'God is against the proud, but he gives grace to the humble.'
James 4:6

Don't be too proud in the Lord's presence, and he will make you great.
James 4:10

'He has brought down rulers from their thrones and raised up the humble.'
Luke 1:52

When Jesus noticed that some of the guests were choosing the best places to sit, he told this story: 'When someone invites you to a wedding feast, don't take the most important seat, because someone more important than you may have been invited. The host, who invited both of you, will come to you and say, "Give this person your seat." Then you will be embarrassed and will have to move to the last place. So when you are invited, go and sit in a seat that is not important. When the host comes to you, he may say, "Friend, move up here to a more important place." Then all the other guests will respect you. All who make themselves great will be made humble, but those who make themselves humble will be made great.'
Luke 14:7–11

Pride will destroy a person; a proud attitude leads to ruin. It is better to be humble and be with those who suffer than to share stolen property with the proud.
Proverbs 16:18–19

your mind

When have I been extremely humiliated?

On a scale of 1–10 how proud am I?

1 2 3 4 5 6 7 8 9 10

What was Jesus' reward for being humble?
(HINT: Philippians 2:5–8)

What is false humility?

HUMILITY

87

BODY SLAM

chipK's mind

Don't you just hate it when you think up a great comeback – five minutes too late? I'm sure you've experienced this before. Someone says something which really offends you, and you want to say something clever back, but what comes out of your mouth just ends up making you look (and feel) even more stupid than before. Then, once it's too late, you start replaying the scenario over and over in your mind, and *bam!* Something brilliant pops up. You think, 'If only I'd said that instead!'

I remember hearing a guest speaker at my youth group teaching on what Christians call 'spiritual warfare' – the unseen battle between good and evil. Basically, he didn't believe any of it. He said that all this shouting at the devil and binding up demons was just a bunch of baloney, and that all we needed to do as Christians was stand there and eventually the devil would go away. And the worst part is, to my utter shock and horror, the rest of my youth group proceeded to agree with him! I was the only one in the room to openly disagree with the man, but as much as I wanted to publicly win my 'case', at the time I couldn't think of anything clever enough to back it up. It was the perfect example of a humiliating comeback.

Needless to say, I went home and did some serious Word-searching on what spiritual warfare is really all about. My dad helped me to see that we're actually engaged in a full-on WWF wrestling match with the devil from the moment we become Christians. Can you imagine what would happen if you just stood there while the Undertaker danced around the ring and charged at you for one final flying body slam? Not a very pretty picture if you ask me. The Bible clearly says that we need to be aware of Satan's secret war tactics, so that when he fires his missiles of temptation at us, we can fire back with atomic bombs of Scripture, reminding him that Jesus is our master, not him.

There's a comeback worth knowing – and not five minutes too late.

God's mind

Our fight is not against people on Earth but against the rulers and authorities and the powers of this world's darkness, against the spiritual powers of evil in the heavenly world.
Ephesians 6:12

I did this so that Satan would not win anything from us, because we know very well what Satan's plans are.
2 Corinthians 2:11

'Since the time John the Baptist came until now, the kingdom of heaven has been going forwards in strength, and people have been trying to take it by force.'
Matthew 11:12

'But if I use the power of God's Spirit to force out demons, then the kingdom of God has come to you. If anyone wants to enter a strong person's house and steal his things, he must first tie up the strong person. Then he can steal the things from the house.'
Matthew 12:28–29

'And our brothers and sisters defeated him by the blood of the Lamb's death and by the message they preached. They did not love their lives so much that they were afraid of death.'
Revelation 12:11

When the 72 came back, they were very happy and said, 'Lord, even the demons obeyed us when we used your name!' Jesus said, 'I saw Satan fall like lightning from heaven. Listen, I have given you power to walk on snakes and scorpions, power that is greater than the enemy has. So nothing will hurt you. But you should not be happy because the spirits obey you but because your names are written in heaven.'
Luke 10:17–20

'I will give you the keys of the kingdom of heaven; the things you don't allow on earth will be the things that God does not allow, and the things you allow on earth will be the things that God allows.'
Matthew 16:19

your mind

When was the last time I failed miserably on a great comeback?

What's my greatest offensive weapon against the devil? (HINT: Ephesians 6:17–18)

What's the biggest temptation I'm 'wrestling' with at the moment?

Two practical things I can do to overcome this temptation are:

1.

2.

REST

chipK's mind

Something I think is vitally important, yet so often overlooked, is having good rest. I'm not just talking about sleep (although it is a very necessary type of rest which I enjoy very much). I'm referring to the kind of rest that God *commands* us to take in the Bible. It's a holy chill-out. It's when we take a deep breath in, and then contemplate the blessings God has lavished on us as we slowly breathe out. He set apart the seventh day of creation, after having made everything in the universe during the first six. He did this as an example for us.

Jesus calls us to find rest in him

Whenever my wife and I take a proper vacation (and trust me, it isn't often enough) we have to be really careful not to allow ourselves to get too busy. Otherwise we end up feeling like we need a vacation from our vacation! Without getting enough serious R & R, we'll end up going back to work just as stressed as we were when we left.

In a world where everything moves at a million miles per hour, Jesus calls us to find rest in him. This is a guy who purposely waited four days to raise his friend Lazarus from the dead. He spent forty days alone in the desert, fasting and being prepared for the ministry God had given him. He even waited thirty years before performing his first miracle!

I guarantee it. You'll feel blessed, refreshed and free from stress when you find rest.

90

God's mind

your mind

'Come to me, all of you who are tired and have heavy loads, and I will give you rest. Accept my teachings and learn from me, because I am gentle and humble in spirit, and you will find rest for your lives. The teaching that I ask you to accept is easy; the load I give you to carry is light.'
Matthew 11:28–30

I find rest in God alone; only he gives me hope.
Psalm 62:5

By the seventh day God finished the work he had been doing, so he rested from all his work. God blessed the seventh day and made it a holy day, because on that day he rested from all the work he had done in creating the world.
Genesis 2:2–3

He lets me rest in green pastures. He leads me to calm water. He gives me new strength. He leads me on paths that are right for the good of his name.
Psalm 23:2–3

God says, 'Be quiet and know that I am God. I will be supreme over all the nations; I will be supreme in the earth.'
Psalm 46:10

Come to me

. . . and I will give you rest

REST

Am I getting enough sleep at night?

Whenever I take time to rest, how do I seriously unwind?

Why is everyone so busy all the time?

What's the difference between being restful and being lazy?

Restful:

Lazy:

TONGUE

chipK's mind

Big things really do come in tiny packages. That's why diamond rings are so expensive. Or take, for instance, a small bullet. In the palm of your hand it's harmless, but in the middle of your head it's lethal. Or even worse, a miniscule little atom. So small it's invisible, but split it in half and you get the biggest explosion mankind has generated in the history of the world (and we've regretted it ever since).

The human tongue is a puny-yet-powerful little device

In the same way, the human tongue is a puny-yet-powerful little device. The Bible has all sorts of things to say about that slimy wet muscle housed just behind the teeth in your mouth. The things you say can either completely destroy a person or totally brighten their day. A lot of people think that foul language only consists of swear words, and as long as they don't use any of those, they're alright. But actually, it includes rude jokes, gossip, lies, deception and hateful comments, which we hear all the time in so-called safe media environments like the radio, daytime television and teen magazines.

We need to start a new trend of genuinely encouraging and building each other up. Guard your words as if they were tiny weapons of mass destruction. Because they certainly can be.

God's mind

We all make many mistakes. If people never said anything wrong, they would be perfect and able to control their entire selves too. When we put bits into the mouths of horses to make them obey us, we can control their whole bodies. Also a ship is very big, and it is pushed by strong winds. But a very small rudder controls that big ship, making it go wherever the person wants. It is the same with the tongue. It is a small part of the body, but it boasts about great things. A big forest fire can be started with only a little flame. And the tongue is like a fire. It is a whole world of evil among the parts of our bodies. The tongue spreads its evil thorough the whole body. The tongue is set on fire by hell, and it starts a fire that influences all of life. People can tame every kind of wild animal, bird, reptile, and fish, and they have tamed them, but no one can tame the tongue. It is wild and evil and full of deadly poison. We use our tongues to praise our Lord and Father, but then we curse people, whom God made like himself. Praises and curses come from the same mouth! My brothers and sisters, this should not happen.
James 3:2–10

A gentle answer will calm a person's anger, but an unkind answer will cause more anger.
Proverbs 15:1

When you talk, do not say harmful things, but say what people need – words that will help others become stronger. Then what you say will do good to those who listen to you . . . Also, there must be no evil talk among you, and you must not speak foolishly or tell evil jokes. These things are not right for you. Instead, you should be giving thanks to God.
Ephesians 4:29; 5:4

But now also put these things out of your life: anger, bad temper, doing or saying things to hurt others and using evil words when you talk. Do not lie to each other. You have left your old sinful life and the things you did before.
Colossians 3:8–9

Wish good for those who harm you; wish them well and do not curse them.
Romans 12:14

your mind

How do I feel when people say bad things about me? And good things?

Do I have a right to return one hurtful comment with another?

How can I genuinely be enthusiastic and encouraging without sounding cheesy?

How do the words I say affect the way I live?

COMMUNION

chipK's mind

Communion is basically just a small meal that Christians eat together in order to celebrate and remember what Jesus did for us on the cross two thousand years ago. It's kinda the same as eating cake with all your mates on your birthday to celebrate the day you were born – only slightly more serious.

Communion is a time to do some serious soul searching

Jesus kicked it all off when he ate the annual Jewish Passover meal with all twelve of his disciples, just before he died. Those guys had eaten that same traditional meal every year of their lives, celebrating the day that the angel of death 'passed over' the homes of their ancestors, allowing the firstborn son of each family to live. (You can read the story in Exodus 11–12.) But Jesus said that from now on, this same annual meal should be eaten for another reason. He was about to go through the most excruciating pain and punishment ever endured by any human being, not because he deserved it, but so that eternal death could 'pass over' *us*.

Taking Communion is also a time to do some serious soul searching in order to sort out any unresolved differences or arguments you've had since the last time you took it. When we remember the love Jesus showed us by going through all that pain in our place, even while we were still offending him, it motivates us to show the same kind of love to the people who've offended us.

Jesus' death meant that we could spend eternity with God in heaven. That's gotta be worth celebrating, just like the first day of your life.

God's mind

When the time came, Jesus and the apostles were sitting at the table. He said to them, 'I wanted very much to eat this Passover meal with you before I suffer. I will not eat another Passover meal until it is given its true meaning in the kingdom of God.' Then Jesus took a cup, gave thanks and said, 'Take this cup and share it among yourselves. I will not drink again from the fruit of the vine until God's kingdom comes.' Then Jesus took some bread, gave thanks, broke it and gave it to the apostles, saying, 'This is my body, which I am giving for you. Do this to remember me.' In the same way, after supper, Jesus took the cup and said, 'This cup is the new agreement that God makes with his people. This new agreement begins with my blood which is poured out for you.'
Luke 22:14–20

Every time you eat this bread and drink this cup you are telling others about the Lord's death until he comes. So a person who eats the bread or drinks the cup of the Lord in a way that is not worthy of it will be guilty of sinning against the body and the blood of the Lord. Look into your own hearts before you eat the bread and drink the cup, because all who eat the bread and drink the cup without recognising the body eat and drink judgment against themselves. That is why many in your group are sick and weak, and many have died.
1 Corinthians 11:26–30

your mind

What does Communion mean to me?

What happened to the Jewish people right after the first Passover? (HINT: Exodus 12:31–42)

How is this significant in Communion?

When/where will I next take Communion?

POWER

chipK's mind

The very first computer game I ever owned was Nintendo's Super Mario Bros. My favourite character was Luigi (probably because he wore green – my favourite colour), and I would spend hours running him through the different levels, bouncing him off the '?' bricks and dodging all the baddies. The best part for me, though, was when the flashing star landed on him. All of a sudden, for about ten seconds, he was totally invincible, smashing through bad guys and running at hyper speed. I can still hear the frantic music in my head – da-da-dum, da-da-da-da-dum . . . That star gave him unstoppable power.

For about ten seconds, he was totally invincible

Now, obviously, computer games aren't exactly the same as real life. We don't jump up and punch random floating boxes or climb never ending vines on the way to work or school, do we? However there is a special kind of *power* that God gives to us when we're filled up with the Holy Spirit. It helps us to smash right through the 'bad guys' we face every day like pride, fear, greed and peer pressure. When our lives are truly handed over to God, we'll even see miracles happening, like people getting saved, healed and delivered from all sorts of traps the devil has caught them up in. I, for one, would much rather catch that kind of power than some flashing star.

Game over.

God's mind

Because the kingdom of God is present not in talk but in power.
1 Corinthians 4:20

'But when the Holy Spirit comes to you, you will receive power. You will be my witnesses – in Jerusalem, in all of Judea, in Samaria and in every part of the world.'
Acts 1:8

I am proud of the Good News, because it is the power God uses to save everyone who believes – to save the Jews first, and also to save those who are not Jews.
Romans 1:16

'And those who believe will be able to do these things as proof: they will use my name to force out demons. They will speak in new languages. They will pick up snakes and drink poison without being hurt. They will touch the sick, and the sick will be healed.'
Mark 16:17–18

With God's power working in us, God can do much, much more than anything we can ask or imagine.
Ephesians 3:20

'When you are weak, my power is made perfect in you.' So I am very happy to boast about my weaknesses. Then Christ's power can live in me.
2 Corinthians 12: 9b

your mind

Why is it that most computer games seem to have an obsession with special powers?

If I could just have one super power what would it be?

When's the last time I was around any miracles?

Is this power that God promises ever really mine at all?

POOR

chipK's mind

You don't have to search very far in God's Word to find that his heart beats for the poor. King David started life as a grubby shepherd boy. Joseph was sold into slavery by his jealous brothers. John the Baptist survived on sticky-grasshopper-pudding for much of his life. Even Jesus himself was poor enough to be born in an extremely unhygienic stable. Yet all of these people were used by God to change the course of history.

I came face to face with blatant poverty while on a ministry trip with my family to Romania. First off, the entire country seemed to smell of hideous body odour. Secondly, I just about passed out after being directed towards a communal outhouse at the back of a broken-down gas station to relieve myself. The stench was so horrific I had to hold my breath, and even still, I could literally taste it on my tongue. Thirdly, I'll never forget stopping at some traffic lights and watching as three sad little kids came over to our car and started wiping our windscreen with dirty oily rags. They stared longingly at us through big hungry eyes as they proceeded to 'clean' our car, actually making it dirtier than it already was! We didn't have any money in their currency yet, so my mom rummaged around desperately and found a small pack of cookies. When she handed it to them through her window, their huge eyes widened even further as if she was handing them the greatest gift they'd ever been given. We watched them as they ran off and formed a huddle in order to divvy up their new-found spoils – a crummy handful of cookies.

Jesus said that the poor would always be with us. But how will we choose to treat them? Can we really get away with ignoring the homeless tramp on the high street? What would Jesus do?

If you ask me, it's time to stop judging and start loving.

God's mind

'You will always have the poor with you . . .' *John 12:8a*

'Then those people will answer, "Lord, when did we see you hungry or thirsty or alone and away from home or without clothes or sick or in prison? When did we see these things and not help you?" Then the King will answer, "I tell you the truth, anything you refused to do for even the least of my people here, you refused to do for me." These people will go off to be punished for ever, but the good people will go to live forever.'
Matthew 25:44–46

Then Jesus said to the man who had invited him, 'When you give a lunch or a dinner, don't invite only your friends, your family, your other relatives and your rich neighbours. At another time they will invite you to eat with them, and you will be repaid. Instead, when you give a feast, invite the poor, the crippled, the lame and the blind. Then you will be blessed, because they have nothing and cannot pay you back.'
Luke 14:12–14a

'The Lord has put his Spirit in me, because he appointed me to tell the Good News to the poor. He has sent me to tell the captives they are free and to tell the blind that they can see again. God sent me to free those who have been treated unfairly.'
Luke 4:18–19

'Those people who know they have great spiritual needs are happy, because the kingdom of heaven belongs to them.'
Matthew 5:3

Story of the Good Samaritan
Luke 10:30–35

your mind

When was the last time I helped out someone who was poor?

What is my first reaction to a homeless person on the high street?

Most people associate being poor with having no money. What are some other ways that people can be poor?

1.

2.

3.

What can I do this week to represent Jesus to someone who's poor?

FIRE PROOF

chipK's mind

Have you ever tried to start a bonfire without matches? Didn't think so. Matches are absolutely vital to every good bonfire. Trust me, Guy Fawkes Night just wouldn't be the same without them. But in the Bible, there are several occasions of *supernatural* fires – matches not included. Take for instance the burning bush that talked to Moses, or the tongues of fire that appeared over the heads of the first Spirit-filled Christians, like a light bulb when someone's got a brilliant idea in cartoons.

One of my favourites, though, is the appearance of a supernatural fire in the famous showdown of Elijah v. the Prophets of Baal. For those seriously deceived prophets, it was like the worst club night ever. They spent all morning shouting, all afternoon dancing, all evening bleeding – and for what? Nothing. No fire from Baal whatsoever. Once Elijah finished mocking them (even suggesting that maybe their god was otherwise engaged on the bog!), he simply said a prayer to the one true God and *wham!* The fire that fell from heaven even burned up the stones and dust underneath the bonfire. Anyone who saw that could not have asked for better proof that God is for real. This was fire proof!

> For those seriously deceived prophets, it was like the worst club night ever

The Bible describes God as a 'consuming fire'. He burns up all the rubbish in our lives. He purifies and refines us by devouring our wrong motives of selfishness, pride and greed in his unquenchable 'flames'. This in turn produces honourable motives like sacrifice, humility and generous love.

All of this, and without even one single match.

God's mind

Story of Elijah v. Prophets of Baal
I Kings 18:25–39

There the angel of the Lord appeared to him in flames of fire coming out of a bush. Moses saw that the bush was on fire, but it was not burning up. So he said, 'I will go closer to this strange thing. How can a bush continue burning without burning up?' When the Lord saw Moses was coming to look at the bush, God called to him from the bush, 'Moses, Moses!' And Moses said, 'Here I am.'
Exodus 3:2–4

When the day of Pentecost came, they were all together in one place. Suddenly a noise like a strong, blowing wind came from heaven and filled the whole house where they were sitting. They saw something like flames of fire that were separated and stood over each person there. They were all filled with the Holy Spirit, and they began to speak different languages by the power the Holy Spirit was giving them.
Acts 2:1–4

Our God is like a fire that burns things up.
Hebrews 12:29

Our God is like a fire that **burns things up**

your mind

What is the difference between a contained bonfire and a house that has caught on fire?

Which of the two examples above is a better picture of the *character* of God? Why?

Three articles of rubbish in my life which need to get burned up in God's bonfire are:

1.

2.

3.

The Bible sometimes describes God as a 'consuming fire'. What are some other *forms* in which God reveals himself in the Bible? [HINT: Acts 2:1–2; Luke 3:21–22]

CHURCH

chipK's mind

A while ago, thebandwithnoname did a gig at York Minster. We had a great time and even had the amazing privilege of meeting the Archbishop of York. I'll never forget the immensity of that ancient church. Our music seemed to reverberate for an eternity as the track echoed past the stained glass windows and up into those gothic high ceilings. Quite a sound!

The church is not a building . . . it's the people inside

The very next day we did an outdoor concert in Birmingham. Just like the York Minster gig, this one was attended by hundreds of young Christians, all of them praising and worshipping God with us. Only this time, instead of being cooped up inside an ancient church, we were right out on the streets, just outside what looked like the town hall or something downtown. As I gazed at the crowd among the urban high-rise buildings, I couldn't help but think that actually this was a better representation of what the early church must've been like and indeed, what church today should look like. A massive group of people enjoying God right out in the open air, while unbelievers and passers-by stared at them, wondering what in the world was going on.

The church is not a building . . . it's the people inside. When Jesus talked about the church he used the illustration of salt bringing out the flavour in food. He also used the example of a bright shining city on a hill.

Let's be the salt and light we're meant to be, flavouring and illuminating the outside world with a message of repentance (turning away from our old sinful lifestyles), grace (accepting the amazing free gift of God's forgiveness) and freedom (living a life totally liberated to do what God wants us to do).

God's mind

'So I tell you, you are Peter. On this rock I will build my church, and the power of death will not be able to defeat it.'
Matthew 16:18

One of those at the table with Jesus heard these things and said to him, 'Happy are the people who will share in the meal in God's kingdom.' Jesus said to him, 'A man gave a big banquet and invited many people. When it was time to eat, the man sent his servant to tell the guests, "Come. Everything is ready." But all the guests made excuses. The first one said, "I have just bought a field, and I must go and look at it. Please excuse me." Another said, "I have just bought five pairs of oxen; I must go and try them. Please excuse me." A third person said, "I just got married; I can't come." So the servant returned and told his master what had happened. Then the master became angry and said, "Go at once into the streets and alleys of the town, and bring in the poor, the crippled, the blind, and the lame." Later the servant said to him, "Master, I did what you commanded, but we still have room." The master said to the servant, "Go out to the roads and country lanes, and tell the people there to come so my house will be full. I tell you, none of those whom I invited first will eat with me."'
Luke 14:15–24

Let them praise his greatness in the meeting of the people; let them praise him in the meeting of the elders.
Psalm 107:32

'You are the salt of the earth. But if the salt loses its salty taste, it cannot be made salty again. It is good for nothing, except to be thrown out and walked on. You are the light that gives light to the world. A city that is built on a hill cannot be hidden. And people don't hide a light under a bowl. They put it on a lampstand so the light shines for all the people in the house. In the same way, you should be a light for other people. Live so that they will see the good things you do and will praise your Father in heaven.'
Matthew 5:13–16

your mind

What is *my* most memorable representation of what church should be like?

How can I shine the 'light' God has placed in me today?

Why does Jesus compare Christians to 'salt'?

How can I be like 'salt' to the people around me?

HEAVEN

chipK's mind

Have you ever wondered what heaven will be like? You know you have. I always ask myself stuff like: 'Will I be able to fly in heaven?' or 'What will we spend all our time doing up there?' or 'What's it going to look like, especially compared to all the beauty we already have down here on earth?'

On a recent trip to the States, my wife and I experienced a taste of heaven when we visited a well-known Christian University. Our mouths literally dropped open the moment we stepped into the main reception. Ever heard the phrase, 'I thought I'd died and gone to heaven'? Well we both nearly pinched ourselves to make sure we actually hadn't! The massive empty hall had bright white marble floors, huge sky blue walls that stretched up and up into eternity, and a chandelier the size of an alien spacecraft. For some reason the entire lobby just happened to be devoid of any humans the second we walked in, so the light bouncing off the ceiling, floor and walls was bright enough to make us shade our eyes. You'd have to see it to believe it. It was 'heaven'.

We'll never really know what heaven is like until we're finally there. Everything we try to imagine with our earthly minds is really just pure speculation. Mansions, crowns, wings. One thing we can be sure of, though, is this: we'll get to see Jesus face to face, and worship him forever. If you ask me, that's going to be the best part of all. Until then, I'll just have to be content with asking questions.

God's mind

Now we see a dim reflection, as if we were looking into a mirror, but then we shall see clearly. Now I know only a part, but then I will know fully, as God has known me.
1 Corinthians 13:12

I know a man in Christ who was taken up to the third heaven fourteen years ago. I do not know whether the man was in his body or out of his body, but God knows. And I know that this man was taken up to paradise. . . . He heard things he is not able to explain, things that no human is allowed to tell.
2 Corinthians 12:2–4

Immediately I was in the Spirit, and before me was a throne in heaven, and someone was sitting on it. The One who sat on the throne looked like precious stones, like jasper and carnelian. All around the throne was a rainbow the colour of an emerald. Around the throne there were 24 other thrones with 24 elders sitting on them. They were dressed in white and had golden crowns on their heads. Lightning flashes and noises and thundering came from the throne. Before the throne seven lamps were burning which are the seven spirits of God. Also before the throne there was something that looked like a sea of glass, clear like crystal. In the centre and around the throne were four living creatures with eyes all over them, in front and behind.
Revelation 4:2–6

The wall was made of jasper, and the city was made of pure gold, as pure as glass. The foundation stones of the city walls were decorated with every kind of jewel. The first foundation was jasper, the second was sapphire, the third was chalcedony, the fourth was emerald, the fifth was onyx, the sixth was carnelian, the seventh was chrysolite, the eighth was beryl, the ninth was topaz, the tenth was chrysoprase, the eleventh was jacinth, and the twelfth was amethyst. The twelve gates were twelve pearls, each gate having been made from a single pearl. And the street of the city was made of pure gold as clear as glass. I did not see a temple in the city, because the Lord God Almighty and the Lamb are the city's temple. The city does not need the sun or the moon to shine on it, because the glory of God is its light, and the Lamb is the city's lamp. By its light the

people of the world will walk, and the kings of the earth will bring their glory into it. The city's gates will never be shut on any day, because there is no night there. The glory and the honour of the nations will be brought into it. Nothing unclean and no one who does shameful things or tells lies will ever go into it. Only those whose names are written in the Lamb's book of life will enter the city.
Revelation 21:18–27

your mind

What is the most beautiful sight I've ever seen?

How does this compare to what I will see in heaven?

Apart from Jesus (too obvious), who's the first person I want to talk to when I get to heaven?

How can I start to experience heaven on earth – even right now? (HINT: John 17:3)

AUTHORITY

chipK's mind

I'll be honest with you. This is the first book I've ever written. I have absolutely no idea how many people will buy it or whether or not the people who do buy it will even enjoy it. But there is one thing I do know: by God's grace and the Holy Spirit's inspiration, I am the author of this book. It didn't just write itself. If someone picks up this book and wonders why one bit comes before another chapter, or why a certain sentence is worded in a particular way, the best person for them to ask is me, Chip Kendall, the author. I suppose that would make me the ultimate 'authority' on this here book . . .

By respecting our authorities, we're respecting Jesus

Okay, before I start to sound too bigheaded, let me get to the point. The Bible says that all authority has been given by God. This means the current president of the United States is only the president because God has made him so. The current prime minister of England has been chosen by God to lead the country of England. Your boss or principal or mother or anyone else who governs your life, has been placed there for a reason. God put them there, as your authority.

We have a responsibility to respect those God has placed over us. No ifs, ands or buts. By respecting our authorities, we're respecting the Lord Jesus. Pray for them. Listen to them. Honour them. After all, you may one day find yourself in a position of authority over someone else.

Or even worse, you might be the author of *your* first book.

God's mind

All of you must yield to the government rulers. No one rules unless God has given him the power to rule, and no one rules now without that power from God. So those who are against the government are really against what God has commanded. And they will bring punishment on themselves. Those who do right do not have to fear the rulers, only those who do wrong fear them. Do you want to be unafraid of the rulers? Then do what is right, and they will praise you. The ruler is God's servant to help you. But if you do wrong, then be afraid. He has the power to punish; he is God's servant to punish those who do wrong. So you must yield to the government, not only because you might be punished, but because you know it is right.
Romans 13:1–5

'I, too, am a man under the authority of others, and I have soldiers under my command. I tell one soldier, "Go," and he goes. I tell another solider, "Come," and he comes. I say to my servant, "Do this," and my servant does it.'
Matthew 8:9

Show respect for all people: love the brothers and sisters of God's family, respect God, honour the king.
1 Peter 2:17

Do what is **right,** and they will praise you

your mind

Who has God placed in a position of authority over me?

How often do I pray for them?

How can I practically show my respect for them?

Today I will honour my authorities by:

This is just an experiment.

If you've read this book all the way through, please send a brief email to the address below telling me what you thought about it – good or bad.

Thanks

chipK
chipk@thebandwithnoname.com

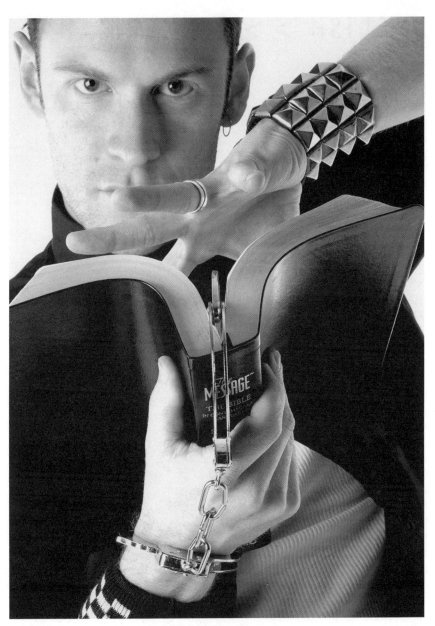

I love God's Word

ENGLISH >>> AMERICAN

ENGLISH	AMERICAN
ad/advertisement	commercial
big up	praise/show respect to
bin/dustbin	trash/trash can
biscuits	cookies
bog	toilet/john
brickin' it	petrified/scared
cheque	check
dosh	cash/money
garden	yard
grubby	dirty
heap/heaps	lots/a lot
head teacher	principal
high street	downtown
holiday	vacation
loo/toilet	bathroom/w.c.
mates	friends
mobile phone	cell phone
mum	mom
naff	dull/bad
pants	underwear
petrol station	gas station
posh	upper class/aristocratic
pudding	dessert
rubbish	garbage/worthless
slushy	slurpee
solicitor	lawyer/attorney
tea/dinner	dinner/supper
text/texting	sms/smsing
top-up card	phone card
tramp	bum
trousers	pants
wheelie bin	back yard trash can
wind up	tease/annoy

innervation's ultimate intention is to make the gospel explode onto the scene in a language that young people can understand and relate to. The dream . . . for every secondary school in the UK to have access to a quality schools' band.

thebandwithnoname and **tbc** are Innervation touring bands. They are responsible for blitzing the world with the Gospel of Jesus Christ, raising the awareness of Innervation, fundraising for Innervation and recruiting young talented people for the schools' bands. These bands are dedicated to their specific counties, doing exciting schools' weeks including: RE lessons, lunchtime concerts, and Friday night events where the young people have an opportunity to respond to the Gospel.

The best thing about Innervation is that it's already working! Thousands upon thousands of young people are hearing about God and responding to his message.

How YOU can get involved...
You too can be a part of this amazing vision! We are looking for young, talented evangelists aged 17+ to join Innervation and be part of the network of schools' bands. If you think you've got what it takes, please email Innervation: info@innervation.org

Innervation depends on both prayer and financial support in order to continue its work. If you would like to become an Innervation supporter, please contact us via our website: **www.innervation.org** or email us directly at the address above.

Free music download

The Mind of chipK just wouldn't be complete without a massive dose of head-spinning music. His *brain* is constantly banging out beats, and anyone who spends a fair amount of time with him knows that his body is always trying to keep up by humming, whistling, beat-boxing and tapping on random objects. Unfortunately, these noises have not (to-date) been recorded.

However, you are more than welcome to **download a free track from thebandwithnoname at the secret link below.**

www.movation.co.uk/tmock1221

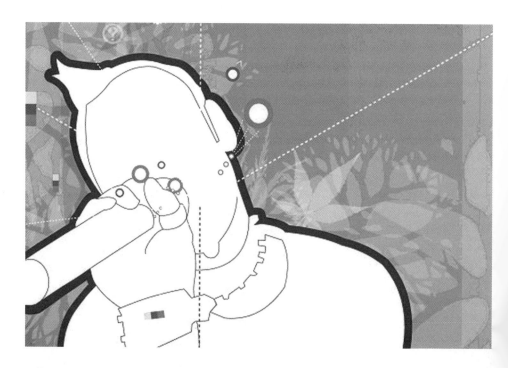